All Over the Map

An Anthology

Kansas Authors Club
District 1
2023

All Over the Map: An Anthology
By District 1, Kansas Authors Club

Copyright 2023 by District One Kansas Authors Club

All Rights Reserved

ISBN: 979-8-218-18420-9

Printed in the USA

Featured Writers

Acknowledgements

When I first walked into the Menninger Room at the Topeka Shawnee County Public Library on a fall day in 2019, the spirit of my mother accompanied me. She would have been a member of this group if she had remained in the area of Kansas where she was born and began her married life. Becoming a member of District 1 of the Kansas Authors Club just felt right. And so it has turned out to be.

When district members proposed publishing an anthology, at first I declined involvement but appointed a committee to explore the issue. I had been elected president of the local group and assumed the position in time to help plan our hosting of the statewide Kansas Authors Club convention. But Covid hit, we began meeting on Zoom, and eventually opted for a virtual event. By the time the convention was over, several of us who had been involved in the planning faced burnout.

But Max Dunavan and Barbara Waters-Peterman stepped up and agreed to take on the task. Thanks to them, the bulk of the work began. As submissions were turned in and edited and as Barbara began designing a cover, I quickly realized the need to get involved in the formatting and publishing process. (Thanks, Mom, for making me such a responsible citizen!)

Thanks, Duane Johnson, for your final proofreading and Carol Yoho for contributing the back cover information. Finally, thanks to all the club members for their suggestions and submissions.

The book you are about to read is truly a showcase for the talented writers who belong to District 1 of the Kansas Authors Club. I am proud to call these writers my friends and colleagues. They have taught me so much in a few short years. We all hope you enjoy the samples of talent in this anthology and find it a true gem in the Kansas writing landscape.

Anne Spry
Kansas Authors Club District 1 President

-6-

Fred C Appelhanz

Writing Poetry

When my mind is amiss
among questions and influences,
my spirit will be dominated
by creativity's insistence.

True emotion will spew forth
with an urgency I cannot ignore.
While words dart about or scream,
my pen feverishly dances.

I know not when poems will surface,
a deluge, overwhelming my mind.
Depriving me of sustenance or sleep,
they know I will succumb.

My petulant, obtuse muse
will declare stark observations.
In words both ardent and anxious,
I revel in being myself.

Poetry is a mistress,
both seductive and demanding.
She declares my inner truth,
in thunderous moments of insight.

Ignoring her enchantment,
I would wither inside.
I won't commit artistic suicide;
I have already tried.

Honey

When a sunset reveals its magnificence,
in wondrous hues and delights,
taking my breath away;
I will whisper your name.

In the stillness of a moonlit night,
enfolding all senses with its serenity,
giving my soul reassurance;
I will whisper your name.

And as life evolves in heartfelt experiences,
capturing moments of incredible clarity,
bringing a smile to my heart;
I will whisper your name.

Or the sound of rain, sight of snowflakes,
reminders of intimate conversations,
causing me to tremble;
I will whisper your name.

The cuddling of lovers' fingertips,
while listening with only their eyes,
witnessing a universe of just two;
I will whisper your name.

Pleasures of consoling assurance,
dwell in your laughter and smile,
when magic stirs the air;
I will whisper your name.

In a baby's eyes, hints of amazing secrets,
or in an embrace of true tenderness,
and in a glancing touch of love;
I will whisper…

When the night is completely silent,
the only sound, one beating heart,
my soul searching for solace;
I will…

This Life

This life…
Time in incremental moments.
Little do we understand
the significance in our choices.
Chaos and serenity intertwine,
like fingers of morning mist.
Hatred and love embrace,
in a symphony of emotions.
This life…
Knows no limits,
Knows no wrong,
Knows no logic,
Only movement.

This life…
Our moment of humanity.
Fleeting are our experiences,
that create who we become.
Cynicism dances with hope,
pirouetting on the abyss.
Loneliness remembers rapture,
in memories of truth.
This life…
Feels no pain,
Feels no regret,
Feels no desire,
Only itself.

This life…
A parade of human spirits.
Cornucopia of encounters,
images in a single atom.
Music holds hands with silence,
lost in each other's heart.
Reality whispers with fantasy;
sharing secrets of ancient riddles.
This life…
Carries our dreams,
Carries our passion,
Carries our meaning,

Morning Love

Whisper sweet sounds,
laced with the emotion
of a thousand kisses.
For my body craves
the esoteric ecstasy
of your touch.

Let the world contract
into a singular moment,
as we drift into
a fog of enchantment.
Safely in infinity's embrace,
all questions disappear.

Time is suspended
within two heartbeats,
beating as one.
Two breaths quiver,
melting into each other,
breathing as one.

Love silently simmers,
as arms and legs enfold
the essence of contentment.
Only intimacy can ignite
passion so genuine,
love so real.

Take Me

Take me comforting breeze,
to where spirits dwell.
Among majestic glaciers,
casting a profound spell.
My soul to contently linger,
amidst wind sculpted artistry.
Crafted by shadowy fingers,
inscribed with runes of mystery.

Take me comforting breeze,
I long for rugged beauty.
Embraced by thunderous clouds,
I experience wonder eagerly.
Comfort within quiet solitude,
awed by Nature's vast grandeur.
Time loosens its dominance,
I wallow in bewitched rapture.

Take me comforting breeze,
be gentle, mysterious and kind.
I crave alluring adventure,
exultation for body and mind.

Moments

Dusk.
Hummingbirds frolic,
Cicadas mesmerize,
Moon ascends quietly.
Tranquility.

Twilight.
Shadows stretch silently,
Fireflies whisper welcome,
Calmness envelopes all.
Euphoria.

Evening.
Whippoorwills harken,
Nighttime's children arise,
Mysteries eagerly stir.
Harmony.

Darkness.
Moon shadows pirouette,
Tree frogs serenade,
Day reluctantly shrugs.
Rapture.

Fred Appelhanz Bio

Fred C. Appelhanz is a poet and a musician, living on 30 acres overlooking a valley. He will tell you, "The valley and its sky, just outside my door, gives me immeasurable sights, sounds and hours of enjoyment, just as does my swing in the old hickory tree. As the years go by, I've learned to open my eyes, ears, and mind to the wonders of Nature and being human."

Having traveled many parts of the western U.S. hiking and camping, his adventure continues with a strong belief that there are many experiences in his future that will be welcomed and admired.

Barbara Brady

HAIKU

Earthworms on sidewalks
Enjoying a rainy day
Please watch where you step

Garden of eggplants
Rows and rows of purple heads
Not a hair on them

Loneliness

"Loneliness and the feeling of being unwanted is the most terrible poverty."

–Mother Teresa (1910-1997)

Loneliness shrouded her like a coat of sweat
on a hot Kansas day. Heat she managed to endure,
but the ache relentlessly penetrating
her bones did not release its grip.
She grabbed her black plastic purse
and headed for Albertson's grocery store,
walking the three blocks to escape
the prison of isolation of her one-room apartment.
She entered the store, grabbed a cart and gripped
the handle to feel a stable surface
to help save her life from dissolving.
She surrounded herself with busy shoppers
but could not confide her secret, knowing
they might laugh at her silliness–a grown woman
grief-stricken because her cat had died–the only
living creature to give her comfort. She traipsed the aisles.

Finally, she grabbed a carton of milk and stood in the checkout line
Ahead of her a small boy with a runny nose begged
his mother in vain for a box of gummy bears. The old woman
fumbled in her purse and held out two crumpled dollar bills.
"Here. Let me buy those for you," she offered.
The boy gave a timid smile and reached for the money.
His warm fingers touched hers.

Words I Want

I want words permanent
as a black panther tattooed
on a biker's arm, words bleach
or age won't pale.
I want words splattered like mustard squirted
across a clean linen cloth
leaving a wake of astonishment,
words that shimmer
pink and pretty as the Prom
Queen's lip gloss, fragile
as her lacy camisole.
I want crazy words crammed
in the laundry basket,
spilled over and kicked
into the corners of the room,
words sturdy as steel beams, sharp
as needles, words unable
to be damaged or diluted.
I want words splashed
like wine on the carpet,
soaking deep into the fibers,
forming a massive maroon stain
that won't wash away.

Bring me brushes
and I will paint
my canvas with words.

Small Request

Student nurses looked forward to the pediatric rotation. Our motherly instincts naturally want to nurture and love children. Given their inborn playful nature, children are delightful patients. Little did I know that my experiences in pediatric nursing would mark my life like indelible black ink splashed on a white uniform.

Our hospital pediatric unit had two parts. One unit cared for infants up to three years old and another unit had the three-year-olds to 16-year-old children. My first assignment was with the babies.

No sooner had I been orientated to the unit when a commotion arose in one of the rooms. Nurses huddled around a green metal crib. I peeked in and saw a tiny child with strands of blonde hair across her damp forehead. Her skin had a strange, greenish-yellow tinge. But the most startling factor was the high-pitched whistling sound that came from her tiny mouth when she gasped for breath. I heard the rattle of suction equipment and saw a nurse run to call the doctor. Something serious had happened.

A short time later, one of the older students told me that Mary, age two, had died of cystic fibrosis. It didn't seem possible that the frail child with the blonde hair I'd seen through the glass partition was dead. I had looked forward to pediatrics with the expectation of playing with the children, reading to them, feeding them, not witnessing a small child dying.

I quickly learned that cystic fibrosis, caused by an inherited defective gene, affects millions of children. This devastating illness causes the body to produce an abnormally thick mucous that clogs the lungs and leads to life-threatening lung infections. This thick mucous also obstructs the pancreas and prevents digestive enzymes from reaching the intestines to break down and absorb food. In the early 1950s, when I was a student nurse, the treatment was limited.

After that devastating experience, my rotation with the babies did not get off to a good start. I remained haunted by the death of Mary. In the face of every child I took care of after that, I saw Mary's sweet face gasping for breath.

After several weeks in the infant part of pediatrics, it was my turn to move to the unit with the older children. Then I met Maggie, Mary's sister. She was five years old. Maggie, too, had cystic fibrosis.

Nurses aren't supposed to have favorite patients, but Maggie soon became mine. I worked the night shift, and fortunately, most of the other children slept. Maggie, however, seldom slept. She was restless and we disturbed her with breathing treatments and frequent medications. In addition, we had to thump on her small back as she leaned over the side of the bed in an attempt to loosen the tenacious mucous that obstructed her air passage. Most of the time Maggie was too weak to do much more than lay in bed propped up by pillows.

Speaking took too much effort, so Maggie didn't say much, but her dark brown eyes spoke volumes. If I asked if she wanted her hair brushed, she raised her eyebrows, nodded ever so slightly, and I knew she meant yes. The cystic fibrosis caused her skin to be rough and itchy so I rubbed her fragile body with soothing lotion. We played "This little piggy…" with her stubby fingers and kept on the overhead light because she didn't like the dark.

The dietician tried to keep Maggie from being malnourished because the pancreatic enzymes needed for digestion couldn't reach her small intestines. But the food had to be sprinkled with oral pancreatic enzymes and didn't taste good. Consequently, when we fed Maggie, she usually choked on the food or vomited. As she got weaker and weaker, she refused most food.

The Christmas holidays approached and Maggie's condition worsened. She was too sick to notice the toys that decorated her crib or the lighted Christmas tree outside her door. One night as I sat with her, Maggie asked for some Jell-O. "I want red," she said. Her voice was barely a whisper.

I scurried to the room where the meal trays were prepared and opened the refrigerator. There was no Jell-O. I hollered to the other nurse that I needed to check the next floor for Jell-O. There were 21 floors in our hospital. I ran upstairs to the next floor. No red Jell-O. I ran to the next. No red Jell-O. I finally found green and yellow, but no red Jell-O. After checking three more kitchens, there was Maggie's red Jell-O.

It didn't take me long to race back to her room. "Sorry, it took me a while. But I found you some red Jell-O," I said. Maggie's eyes brightened. She raised her head while I spooned small bites of Jell-O into her dry mouth.

That was the last time anyone fed Maggie. She died the next day.

Since that experience seventy years ago, I have administered life-saving medications to patients. I have dispensed thousands of pills. I have served Holy Communion. I have fed the hungry at soup kitchens. But never will I provide anything as significant as the red Jell-O I gave that night to Maggie.

Barbara Brady Bio

Barbara Brady says her only claim to fame as a writer is several stories published in *Chicken Soup for the Soul* books. However, her greatest joy is eight grandchildren and twelve great grandchildren.

Marcia Cebulska

The Blacksmith

My great-grandmother was a blacksmith. That's right, a blacksmith. And we're not just talking horseshoes here. My mother's mother's mother hammered gates, chains, and sickles out of red-hot metal. She forged tools for the villagers and carriage wheels for the lord of the manor, the *Pan*.

Me? Some people call me a wordsmith. I metaphorically hammer sentences and paragraphs out of inky shapes on the page. Typing on my computer keyboard, I move prepositions and semi-colons around in the hopes that I can end up with a play or a story somebody might be willing to read.

My foremother went on to birth twelve children. It was the 19th Century in what is now Poland but then was under Austrian rule. She and her family lived in a two-room house under a feudal economy in which it was a crime to take a fish from a stream or a wild berry from a bush. The lord of the manor had the absolute right of life or death over his subjects.

In my spacious Victorian home, I complain that the air conditioning doesn't do a very good job of cooling my writing room. I gave birth to one single child. I eat raspberries and yogurt from the supermarket for breakfast and I have the right to vote.

My mother's mother's mother learned to forge wagon wheels and axe blades from her father who was paid by the *Pan* largely in vodka, a drink that made him less and less able to ply his trade. She learned well and went on to teach smithery to the man who would become my great-grandfather. Passing through her village on his way to Hamburg where he planned to board a ship to America, he'd been looking for a few days' work. He had a substantial moustache, played the concertina, and sang. He stayed a lifetime. Together, my great-grandparents labored and sang their hearts out. Worked long hours and danced with their children. They never made it to America, but their daughter Wiktoria (Victoria in English), my future grandmother, shipped off from Hamburg and headed to the U.S.A. to become a guest worker when she was fifteen.

When I was about to leave for a leisure trip to Europe, my grandmother told me the story of her blacksmith mother. It made me want to visit Dębica. I traveled during the time of Soviet Russian domination. Long lines of hopeful customers stood for hours in front of butcher shops, where only one or two links of sausage hung from hooks. In the few dress stores that were open, exactly one style was displayed: long, black, plain. It was a time of privation but as I strolled the dusty footpaths, I reminded myself that I was walking in my foremothers' footsteps.

My grandmother's brother Franciszek and his family opened their home to me. A hand-painted tiled stove heated the house and produced huge quantities of edibles. Despite the environment of deprivation and hunger, my great-aunts and cousins hosted me with baked hams and filled dumplings, stews, and cheeses. It was clear that they had to beg, borrow, and steal to obtain the provisions. They had traded beloved objects on the black market to cover the tables with food and drink. I was the first and only of my great-grandmother's American descendants to visit.

When I sat down at the groaning table, the women of the family stood behind the chairs, ready to refill the plates. If one spoonful of mashed potatoes was eaten, two more spoonsful replaced it. I had to leave my plate overflowing for my hosts to know that I was satisfied. No Clean Plates Club at that table. A smiling great-uncle played the fiddle. Another, the concertina. Everyone sang and laughed. The room was filled with joy and borrowed abundance.

Having grown up in an immigrant neighborhood, I knew a smattering of Polish. In a garbled version of my great-grandmother's tongue, I asked about her. My relatives were delighted to tell me about her smithy. It was still in the family. They were so glad I asked. The great-uncle who had played the fiddle pointed to himself with a smile. He, yes, he still plied the trade. He led a procession of family members to his home about a mile away, where custom demanded that we sit down to dine once again. When I was seated at the table, he showed me a large, framed photograph of my great-grandparents surrounded by eight of their children. It was the first time I'd seen their likenesses.

After the second dinner, I followed my blacksmith great-uncle down a well-worn path behind the house to an old stone building. He unlatched and swung open the double doors. Sunlight illuminated a cave-like room with ancient uneven walls. I faced a carved stone table that stood at the height of an altar, its surfaces rounded off by time like stones in a stream. Above it was a large opening, like that of the bread oven in my parents' bakery, covered with a patina of centuries' old soot, shiny as a new black shoe. I tried to picture my great-grandmother wielding a hot hammer, sweating over the anvil but I failed. In the photograph I had just seen of her, she was a small, slender, gentle-looking woman dressed in her Sunday best. Nevertheless, I had to wipe tears off my cheek. I could feel her in my bones.

Marcia Cebulska Bio

Marcia Cebulska has received the Dorothy Silver Award, the Jane Chambers International Award, Kansas Arts Commission Master Artist Fellowships, and other honors for her playwriting and screenwriting. Her work has been performed at thousands of venues worldwide and aired on PBS. A member of The Dramatists Guild and a Fellow of the Center for Kansas Studies, Marcia has been writer-in-residence at The University of Georgia, Mary Anderson Center for the Arts, Marion College and The William Inge Center for the Arts. Marcia's novel, *Watching Men Dance,* was published in 2020 and her non-fiction book *Skywriting* was released in 2019. Marcia lives in Topeka.

Annabelle Corrick

Change of Venue

Alana Fitzgerald had been missing for five weeks. Her mother Estelle remained frantic as did Alana's boyfriend Matt. They arranged to meet with Alana's best friend Lynn to compare notes and to strategize. Estelle thought the police had let the case grow cold as an iceberg, barely touching its tip.

In a corner of the Midwestern college town's busiest coffee shop, Estelle spoke in hushed tones: "Let's go over what we know of her final moments that Friday. We might have overlooked something. Matt, you were the last one to see her."

"That's right." He fumbled his coffee cup to the table, his handsomely fine features contorted in distress. "We had just taken the last of our final exams. I asked her to lunch, but she'd already promised to eat with Lynn and then they'd go shopping."

"But she never showed!" Lynn exclaimed.

"So, Matt." Estelle leveled a piercing blue stare into his gray gaze. "Did you walk Alana to her car, or did you two part ways at the building?"

"Sure, I walked her to her car. I planned to propose that day—a double celebration after finishing college. I had the engagement ring in my pocket."

Lynn nearly choked on her latte. "Oh, really? I'm her best friend and she never gave me a hint."

Matt winced, while a flash of pain crossed Estelle's face. She fingered her perfectly-coiffed hair. "That engagement would have given her ... and everyone such joy."

"I thought she'd really go for it," Matt agreed. "Especially after Cameron split the scene."

"And rightly so," Estelle huffed. Her youngest and loveliest daughter dating that ne'er-do-well? "But we're all so glad he's serving his country in the military."

"Yes, Cameron sure did take off," Lynn put in. "He couldn't wait to leave! My boyfriend almost enlisted with him. I'm so glad Nick—"

"Matt, how was she when you last saw her at her car, before she headed out to meet Lynn?" Estelle inquired.

"Fine. Just seemed on a trot to get to their lunch and go shopping."

"And the lunch was set for what time?" Estelle asked Lynn.

"Around one."

She turned to Matt: "And when did you leave the classroom?"

"It was a tough final in European History. We both stayed to the end, eleven fifty."

"Where were you to meet?" Estelle shot back to Lynn.

"At the Red Fox Café."

"Matt, did you see her drive away?"

"Yeah, I stood there for a while. I couldn't believe I'd missed my chance to propose. We'd been hanging out a lot after morning classes. We'd go over to Dinah's Diner by campus for lunch."

"But this time she hurried off to someplace else. Did you mention that change to the police?" Estelle asked.

"Really hadn't thought of it that way. Say—"

"What?"

"If Alana was going to the Red Fox Café west of campus, I wonder why she turned east from the lot instead of west."

"Ha! That's something." Estelle lurched forward, her eyes gleaming. "Maybe she wasn't planning to meet Lynn at all." Her focus blurred, and although she turned as if to view the motley, small-town groups sipping and slurping their caffeine drinks; she saw only the hope of the single clue.

That evening while Estelle prepared dinner, she imagined a return to normalcy. She had already known that Matt was about to propose—after he confided in his father who then told his mother who then phoned Estelle and excitedly spilled the news. The big scare that Alana and Cameron might run off together ended after Cameron joined the Army. Alana appeared stunned at first but bounced back very well. She got back with her previous boyfriend Matt—the more-than-perfect designated hitter in the game, as her husband Wayne might say.

Two bone-in rib eye steaks sizzled and popped in the fry pan. Estelle grabbed the spatula and flipped them over. She tested the vegetables steaming in their pot, found them tender, and turned that burner off. With the finalization of the dinner's main course, her mind wandered in an effort to think where her youngest daughter might have gone on her own. Undoubtedly Alana had guessed the proposal from Matt was at hand. Maybe such a commitment to Matt posed too quick a turn-around from her involvement with Cameron. She might have needed time alone to sort things out.

But where? Estelle racked her mind to think of past getaways. Various summer camp locales came to mind. Surely that was it. Alana would be back soon! With rising spirits, Estelle went over to the household desk and pulled out the invitation list. She'd advised Matt's mother that the wedding should be soon, considering that Alana was on the rebound. Word came back for a date shortly after their graduation ceremony.

The front door opened. "Hey!" Wayne called heartily from the foyer. In a family of females, Estelle enjoyed how he stood out like a large stag in a forest of does. She smiled, closed the drawer, and went back to the stove. Wayne had been such a rock through it all, never letting Alana's disappearance get him down or giving up hope.

"I found some great wine to go with these steaks," she called back to him. "And I've got some news."

Wayne hurried into the kitchen. "News about Alana? Great. What is it?"

"Not a breakthrough or anything. In fact, I was going to wait until after dinner, but it just slipped out."

Wayne leaned against the kitchen table. "I thought about talking with the police again today, but they always say they'll tell us as soon as—"

"It's not news from the police."

"Oh?" Wayne sat down while she dished up the meal and poured the wine.

"No, just something I got from Matt and Lynn." She took her place at the table. "Looks like Alana might have had some agenda of her own that day. She went the opposite direction she should have gone from the campus lot. Instead of going west to meet Lynn at the Red Fox Café, she turned east. I'm thinking maybe she took off for some time by herself. You know, to think things out. Probably at one of those summer-camp lakes she enjoyed so much."

Wayne smoothed butter onto his potatoes while she spoke, cut some pieces of steak, and began to eat. He then stopped to reply: "Nope, we turned in a list of all her old haunts, including summer camps. Don't you remember?"

"Did we?" Things had been such a blur in the first shock of it all.

"We did, and they've all been checked out." Wayne shook his head. "Knowing Alana, she probably went on some little errand first." He picked up his glass of wine and drank most of it down.

"Yes, that might be true." Estelle's glimmer of hope faded. "It could explain the extra time. The class ended at 11:50, and the lunch was to be at around one."

"You're really delving into details."

"Somebody has to," she asserted. "The police aren't getting anywhere. It's been five whole weeks."

"Don't I know it," Wayne replied. "I've been after my old buddy, Dan Jones. He promised to keep checking with Missing Persons even though he works in Narcotics—and even though these are very busy times for him. They've just done a big drug bust."

"If he's so successful there, I wish he would transfer to Missing Persons. One problem has been solved with Cameron out of the picture—"

"And that was nothing easy." Wayne sighed deeply.

"Nothing easy?" Estelle held her fork in mid-air. "What do you mean?"

"What do you think? You were so upset. Did you expect me to just roll over and play dead—while Alana threw herself away on some nothing gas station grease monkey?"

Estelle's fork clattered onto the table. "What did you *do*?"

Wayne shrugged his shoulders and kept eating, talking between bites. "Nothing much. He wasn't getting the message, so I just told him I'd smash his you-know-whats to bits."

Estelle struggled for words and sputtered: "I … I'm sure he knew you'd do no such thing to anyone."

"You think I said it like some namby? Anyway, he darned well knew he'd better scram." Wayne drank the last drops of his wine. "I hope you're right about Alana maybe taking off on her own. That means she'll soon come to her senses and be back any day now. Where else could she go that we haven't thought of?"

"I don't know," Estelle stared at the dinner she had hardly touched. "Even the search for her car got no results."

"Now that does surprise me." Wayne raised his brows. "Alana was always a smart kid. But successfully ditching her car everyone is looking for? That bright yellow jaguar we gave her? I doubt it." He pushed his plate aside and poured himself more wine. "How about Lauren and Lilly? Will they be dropping by this weekend?"

"Yes. I can't wait to see the twins."

"Right. Think about them."

Estelle nodded. Naturally, she had tried to focus on her older daughters, but she never needed to worry about that sensible pair. "I just hope Alana hasn't come to any harm."

Wayne re-capped the wine bottle. "I hope not too. But Dan thinks that's possible, and that we should start to face it."

Alana dodged in and out of traffic driving an ordinary, beige Camry. The eastern city would take some getting used to with its high-density population where nobody knew anybody. She pulled up into the drive of her town home and glanced down the long row, each front barely distinguishable from the others.

Her new job was dangerous, but so what? Cameron didn't really love her, and her parents couldn't wait to marry her off to safe, boring Matt. Those numbing nuptials had been planned since beyond forever but would never happen. She wouldn't be safe in any respect anytime soon. She didn't want to be. The drug bust had gone well, no one suspecting her involvement. With that and other basic training done, her work would get more wide-ranging. If Cameron could be helping his country, so could she.

Climbing the concrete steps to the stoop, she took out the key, unlocked the door and pushed it open. Aromas of fresh paint and varnish greeted her. She would bring in her few belongings later. Alana glanced at the foyer mirror, initially puzzled, and then pleased by the face looking back at her. Her dark hair now matched her eyes. The short, loose strands distracted from her features. She barely recognized her new, bland self.

Walking into the living room, Alana found a large, wing-backed chair and eased into it. Good to relax a moment after the long trip. There had been two urban centers to navigate around before she reached this one. She'd had plenty of time during the two-and-a-half-day trip to think. Although excitement continued to tingle through her nerves, occasionally she had wondered …

Sleep overcame her consciousness for hours, or maybe only minutes before her phone rang, jolting her awake. Adrenaline rushed through her, and she sprang up. Alana listened carefully to the instructions.

Yes! Time to report for her CIA special ops assignment.

Annabelle Corrick Bio

Annabelle Corrick has been a member of the Kansas Authors Club, District One, for a dozen years, serving in a couple of terms as secretary. In the state Literary Contest, she was the 2015 Prose Writer of the Year. Her writing has appeared in _Twisting Topeka_ Community Novel, _105 Meadowlark Reader_, and other publications.

Roger K. Droz

The Pool Hall

"Pool Hall" were the only two words on the front of the old building. They hung high up on the yellowish metal siding facade of the old two-story. Two distinct words, in large brown plastic letters, fastened sloppily. One of the O's had come unfastened at the top and lay against the L. They covered the original hand-painted nearly illegible letters which also, spelled "Pool Hall." Years before, when I was a kid, there had been a metal awning that extended from the building to the street, but that had been torn off, leaving only the cast iron fittings bolted to the concrete and a rusted angle iron strip where it had fastened to the wall.

If you were to look in the phone book (I never did) you might find the phone number under *Fairfield Pool Hall, Jefferson County Pool Hall, Wink and Goldie's Place*, or something altogether different. All I knew was, that if you spoke the words "Pool Hall," as in "Mom, I'm going to the Pool Hall," (words I never spoke), the recipient of those words would know your exact intended destination.

Fairfield had three pool halls at that time. One in the area known as New Chicago, and one in the West End. The clientele of the three was distinctively different. The pool hall in New Chicago had its brand of customers, fighters. We regularly heard of fights breaking out there. Fights often started inside the hall and would spread outside, sometimes even into the street. Cops were seen regularly patrolling the area, just in case. The West End pool hall catered to only one type of customer, West Enders. If you weren't a West Ender, you weren't welcome there, or any other place in the West End for that matter. And if you weren't a West Ender, you didn't want to go to the West End, for anything, anyway.

The Pool Hall downtown, the one I frequented, had the best clientele, serious pool players. It stood just off the square, across the street from the Hunt Hotel, which at the time, was Fairfield's bus stop. Me and my buddy Lunk liked to lean our bikes against the side of the building and share the benches in front of the hall with some of the regulars; old guys, young guys, retired guys, pool players taking a break, and an assortment of ne'er do wells, all of whom sat for hours discussing the price of corn and beans and any other earth-shaking affairs in need of correction while chomping on the last of their unlit cigars. Silence came over the benches with the first hum of the bus's engine when it downshifted as it began to approach the hotel. Then, quietly, we watched the bus jerk uncomfortably to a stop, and open its door with a swoosh. In unison, we strained to examine each rider as they departed before peering at the others as they emerged from the hotel lobby and boarded for parts unknown.

Lunk and I soon discovered they served sandwiches inside the hall, so with paper-route money in our pockets, we ventured in. Thus, my pool hall life began.

There were only three worn concrete steps up to the shrine where local players of repute hung out. I hoped someday to be one of them. A huge solid oak door hid this place of worship, or local den of iniquity, depending on your point of view, from the outside world. For me, it was the former.

Many years of pool sharks (and drunks) entering and leaving the hall had worn indentations in the steps. Once you negotiated those three steps, you had only to push open the heavy door, to enter a world like no other. I felt like I was entering a cathedral. A feeling I should have had upon entering our church, but never quite did; much to my mother's dismay.

The pool hall cathedral was a long skinny room with a high ceiling. It must have been fifteen feet to the ornate filthy square metal panels above, slightly camouflaged by the cigarette haze, which gently swayed each time the front door opened. Lights hung from long cords. Cords so long they held the shrouded incandescent fixtures only three feet above each table. Above the light, a long wire, fastened to the wall on either side, hung with a number of abacus-like wooden spools. To the right was a long wooden bar, lined with old wooden stools; a solid brass foot rail ran its length. Drinkers, a collection of everyone from businessmen in suits, to factory workers, to the professionally unemployed, randomly shared the stools. Social status was ignored here. In front of the drinkers, the long oak bar was littered with beer mugs and whiskey glasses in various stages of fullness. Shelves of beer mugs, shot glasses, and whiskey bottles, organized surprisingly neatly, fronted a large mirror that ran the length of the bar. Behind the bar stood a disturbingly slender worn dark-skinned man. With a sliver of a mustache and slick black wavy hair combed straight back, every hair perfectly groomed, he stood, leaning against the back of the bar with an ever-present smile waiting to refill a drink or greet a new customer.

To the left were three pinball machines. Although often occupied, the constant clatter of bells and bumpers never caught my interest – you put money in them, but never get any back. I couldn't see the point.

Three snooker tables were first in a long line of pool tables that ran the length of the room. Behind them were approximately eight pool tables. On the right, stick racks and small shelves with talcum spools, and numerous chunks of blue chalk lined the walls. On the left, there was a platform about four feet wide and a foot high that started just past the pinball machines and stretched to the rear wall. On the platform sat a row of wooden high-back pool chairs, some with arms, some not. The chairs were always about half occupied with opponents, nervously fingering their cues, waiting their turn at the table.

All this was shrouded in the gray-white haze from many, many cigarettes.

The bartender's name was Wink. As I entered, Wink would smile, wink, and offer his same well-worn greeting, "What's your pleasure?" A tall, always smiling man, stooped at the shoulders, no doubt from years of leaning over beer coolers and bar sinks. If it weren't for his pencil mustache, coal-black, slicked back, wavy hair, white pressed shirt, buttoned to the top, with a worn dark blue bow tie, you might think he was once a farmer who had spent his first lifetime walking beans. In Wink's case, his stoop was certainly from years of leaning down to wash empty beer glasses and refill (draw) new ones, not walking beans.

I pictured Wink, with his height and broad shoulders, as a former high school football player. A defensive back, probably. Though I doubt Wink's wink, accompanied by that broad grin, intimidated many offensive linemen, running backs, or quarterbacks.

This brings me to Goldie. Goldie and Wink were brothers. Goldie shared his height, both were six-three, but nothing else. Goldie was named for his golden hair. He was a thick man, except for the hair. I figured Goldie was an offensive lineman in high school, probably a tackle. I imagined the two brothers, lined up against each other in football scrimmages. I pictured the outcome of every play, Goldie, with his massive farm boy hands and arms, always the winner against Wink's slender childlike arms and piano player hands. Goldie never smiled. The two brothers could hardly be less alike.

Goldie was our neighbor. One of his sons, his youngest, known as Swany, has been mentioned many times previously as a fellow co-conspirator in some of our younger adventures. Early in my pool playing career, I learned the hours Wink and Goldie worked and tried to frequent the hall during Wink's hours. First, because I liked him better, and second, because the less Goldie knew about my pool hall days, the less he could relate, through his wife, to my mother.

I would gradually come to realize that this fear was unfounded. Separated by religion, these two women shared nothing more than residential proximity. And, based on their beliefs, they would not share stories of my pool hall days in the afterlife, because there, they would no longer share a proximity.

Early on, Lunk and I would answer Wink's question, "What's your pleasure?" with "I want a bologna sandwich with mustard and a Coke."

Wink would answer, "You'll have to take it outside, you can't sit at the bar to eat."

Now I know a bologna sandwich doesn't sound like much, but these were special. Wink would open the refrigerator, take out a ring of bologna, cut four one-inch-thick slices, and throw them on the flat top to warm. He removed a hamburger bun from a paper bag, opened it, slathered a gob of butter on each half, and laid the two halves face down next to the bologna. Once the bologna was warm on one side, he turned the slices over, flopped a big chunk of yellow cheese on them, and waited. Once the cheese began to melt, he scooped up the bologna-cheese pile and put it on one half of the bun. Then he opened a gallon jar of whole dill pickles, sliced one in half long ways, laid the two halves on the cheese bologna mixture, covered this ecstasy with the top, rolled it in a sheet of waxed paper, and with a smile and a wink say, "Here you go."

Later, after much badgering, I learned the bologna was made by "a farmer up north somewhere," and the cheese came from a local dairy, "They make it special, just for us," Wink said. The buns came fresh every morning from George's Bakery (which was just up the street), and the pickles were made by "someone's grandmother." All those sources remain a mystery to me to this day. I can only say, "I've never eaten a bologna sandwich that even comes close to those made at the pool hall."

After finishing my public education career, and still living at home, I entered the local institution of higher learning, Parsons College. I had no real direction; the closest thing I had to an aspiration, was, that I wanted to be a teacher. The difference between high school and college was dramatic. In college, they expected you to learn, participate, and excel, but I wasn't interested in any of those.

So, one day, when I should have been studying, I was sitting at the end of the bar (still underage) eating a bologna sandwich, sipping a coke, and talking to Wink. This guy, Sam Smith, came up to me and asked if I'd like to play a game of snooker.

I'd seen him in here before, playing pool or pinball, but never snooker.

"I don't play," I answered.

"Neither do I, but I want to learn. Come on, let's play."

This short concise conversation would prove to be profound, and life-altering.

The table was set up, and ready for play. The red balls were racked, with the eight-ball inside them. The rest of the numbered balls sat in various spots on the table. Sam and I each picked a cue from the racks; he broke, and we began to shoot random balls, picking the easiest shots. The first thing I noticed was that a snooker table is bigger than a pool table, and the pockets are smaller, and a different shape too. You couldn't blast a ball toward the pocket and have it go in. The smaller rounded pockets repelled balls that were approaching too fast.

The snooker learning curve is steep, and our interest began to wane.

After ten minutes of ineffectiveness, Wink came over, "You have to shoot a red ball first. If you make one, you can shoot any numbered ball. The red ball you made stays in the pocket and the numbered ball comes back to its original spot. Once you make all the red balls, you play rotation on the numbered balls. Now, the numbered balls stay down until they are all gone. That's how the game ends. The key in snooker is to leave your opponent without a good shot if you miss. Hand me your cue, I'll show you how to play leave."

Sam and I stood in awe as Wink made several balls in succession, then left the cue ball stymied behind a numbered ball. "Here, your shot," he said, handed Sam back his cue, and winked."

I learned a life lesson that day—*Always know your opponent.*

Sam and I soon became regulars. We met Saturday mornings at 10 o'clock. We learned there was a snooker table hierarchy—beginners play the back table. Players on the middle table watch you and once a middle table player thinks you are good enough (and wants a game against a patsy) they will invite you to play on the middle table. Once you establish yourself as a middle table player, you advance to the front table by invitation only.

Saturday mornings were busy; sometimes it was hard to get a table. So, Sam and I began to play Wednesday evenings too. Mornings on Saturdays were no longer enough, so soon we were playing all day. Wednesday evenings began to start earlier, and last longer.

Play on the front table for the good players only lasted a few hours Saturday mornings. At noon, one o'clock at the latest, players began to move from the tables to the bar for a bologna sandwich and a beer. When lunch ended, most players left the hall. Those who stayed behind settled into an afternoon of drinking and shooting the bull.

My progress was slow, it took me over a year, and a significant amount of money to become a first table player. In the process, I left Sam behind, he just couldn't move up from the middle table, and increasingly, would sit at the bar and drink.

As I moved into my third year of college, a miracle I lasted that long, I met and married Margo. She was another miracle, and snooker began to take a back seat.

Then, mysteriously, yet another miracle; Margo became pregnant, and we had a daughter. In a flash, my life changed. Parenthood brought responsibilities.

I quit Snooker cold turkey; left my cue locked in the rack, and never went back.

I go back to Fairfield occasionally now. My sister still lives there. The Pool Hall is gone, and a restaurant has taken its place. I went there once with some classmates when I was home for a reunion. Now, it is one of those Yuppie-type places that focus as much on the atmosphere as they do their food.

The snooker tables are gone, replaced by an assortment of round and square tables and booths with moronic table cloths perfectly folded linen napkins, and "fresh-cut" fake flowers. The cue racks, talcum spools, and blue chalk have all vanished; replaced by abstract posters. The pinball machines are gone too; a foyer (now pronounced *foyeah*) has taken its place. A lowered ceiling is painted a garish green. Wink's bar is still there; The shot glasses, beer mugs, and whiskey bottles have been replaced with an assortment of specially shaped glasses. Now the barkeeper (barista I suppose) serves fruit-herb concoctions, la de da teas, and status seeker coffees.

The current owners have created a new atmosphere, but it's not my atmosphere. I prefer to remember the pool hall of my youth. I wish I'd never walked through that heavy oak (now painted maroon) door. I can still sense the decades of wear beneath the fresh paint.

I look back now at the existence of, the need for, pool halls. Yes, I think of the aforementioned cafe, with its ambiance or aura, and compare it to that which was the pool hall.

First, let me choose the adversaries. On the one side, we have restaurants, cafes, grocery stores, laundromats, clothing stores, shoe stores, computer stores, big box stores, and more. On the other side, we have places of ill repute, dens of iniquity, if you will, taverns, bars, and pool halls. One goes to a restaurant, shoe store, computer store, etc. to make a purchase. While making said purchase, the customer is always cognizant, that once their transaction is complete, they are going to return to the "real" world.

Bars, taverns, and pool halls are different in that their customers are not making plans to leave as they enter these establishments. Well, they might have promised a spouse or a friend they would meet them at some specified time in the future, but they were lying when they said that, knew they were lying, and felt no remorse as they spoke. They were only thinking about the atmosphere, (definitely not ambiance) inside. I used to wonder, like on a sunny warm Spring day, when driving past a bar, tavern, or pool hall, "Don't they know what they are missing? Wouldn't they be happier outside in the fresh air?"

The answer, of course, is "No."

They don't care what they are missing. Being outside in the fresh air would put them back in the real world. A world full of pressures to address, decisions to be made, bills to be paid, and annoying spouses to deal with. No, they are content to be in a bar. Hopefully, one that serves bologna sandwiches, with bologna "made by a farmer up north somewhere,"

I want to push that heavy door open one more time, have Wink smile, wink, and ask, "What's your pleasure?"

"I'll have a bologna sandwich with mustard, and a Coke."

Roger K. Droz Bio

Roger K. Droz was born and raised in Fairfield, Iowa. He graduated from Parsons College with a BA in History and Political Science. He came to writing late, wishing to write a memoir for his children, grandchildren, and great-grandchildren, telling them what life was like growing up in a small Midwestern town in the 1950s and '60s. His youth.

Roger had a short story, "Bikes and Basketball," published in *Our Iowa Magazine*. Another short story, "First Beer" was the winner of the creative nonfiction category in the *2016 Kansas Voices Contest*. Both are from his memoir, *Growing Up Baseball, Memories, and Mischief*. His flash fiction story, "Thermals" was published in the 2022 50th Anniversary edition of Washburn University's *Inscape* Magazine. This story, "The Pool Hall" is also from his memoir.

Alice Dunavan

Changes for All Seasons

Spring
The sun is happier when nights wane.
Leaf buds are opening slowly to the rain
As brightly blossoms burst abloom
For Spring cleaning, dust off the broom.

Birds flap in from their Southern vacation,
Then eggs hatch and bird songs awaken.
Plant your seeds for new growth,
Earthworms and sunshine, you must have both.

Summer
Days are stretching further now
To ripen as much fruit as time will allow
Explore nature and you will learn
Of concert cicadas and how fireflies burn.

Barefoot children wildly run,
More daylight for having fun
The season of the sun will set fast,
Tomorrow all this will be in the past.

Autumn
Leaves like feathers falling,
The hard frost is calling.
The moon grows bolder
While the days grow colder.

When the birds fly south,
We bring pumpkin pies to mouth.
Squirrel away the reaping,
The bears will soon be sleeping.

Winter
Snowflakes blizzard over town
For Joyous children to sled down
Jazz up in everything gaudy
For Winter comes to everybody.

Warming up fireside at day's end,
Candy canes, cocoa, and marshmallows blend.
Den with family above ground or below,
Imagine what will come after the snow.

Alice Dunavan Bio

Alice Dunavan is a ten-year-old Kansas Authors Club member, author, and poet living with her family and pet chihuahua in Overland Park, Kansas. She enjoys Girls Scouts, mathematics, reading, art, football and learning to play the violin.

Max (Myron) Dunavan

A Place to Go

At some point Ethel might have had a choice. She may have been unaware. She may not have known when she crossed the threshold. Perhaps the change was not sudden, but like a day trip or a dream.

Maybe it was like several dreams, and given the ability to go, she finally, metaphorically speaking, packed her bags and went. I'd like to think that's the way it was—only happiness there.

I'd like to think that there is another reality, a place of safety and promise to which we could each escape when it gets rough. A place to go when the pleasures of living here become too bleak to contemplate any longer.

Ethel slipped into his arms and experienced the joy of young love where there was excitement and passion. She went there often at first just to escape and feel like a whole woman once again.

She would slip back to address the issues of her adult life, but more and more she was slipping off to join her lovers and then there was the baby and then another. Well, she had them to take care of, just how could she continue to go back and forth? She finally stayed permanently, wrapped in the busy life of being a lover and a mother. And how strange she must have found that: a case of deja vu.

Hadn't she done this all before? Hadn't she had a lover and babies? She would ask her mother, of course, but would her mother understand? She could ask her father, but was he angry about her choice of a man and the baby? At times she would fret and wring her hands. Then the baby got sick, the second baby, and he died.

She would cry and cry during the day and the night for her dead baby. Next came the war and she waited and watched for Jim's letters. She kept them on her dresser. Ethel did not have her glasses and could not quite read them, but she would sometimes hold them close to her chest.

Then came the letter she did not want, and she cried, because Jim was dead, dead in some place she had never heard of and couldn't pronounce.

And she cried again, she cried every day. Some would try to console her, and she hoped she could forget. She was so worried after that and would never let her older child out of her sight.

Once he wandered off to find candy and she became distraught. Her child was fine, and she cried when she found him there by the candy counter. He was not naughty, just adventuresome.

This was a stressful life, supporting two children with no husband. Occasionally there was this shimmering mirror in which she could see reflected a wrinkled old woman crying and rocking.

It frightened her and she had lost track of what the mirror was supposed to be. She turned her chair and rocked her child to sleep. Laying him on the bed carefully, she covered him and stepped quietly to the door. Lunch was nearly ready. Lunch was something she looked forward to. She hoped for ice cream. Ethel headed down the hall and she sat at one of the tables alone.

Someone asked her to move, and she was quite bewildered. Someone she did not know said, "Over here is your place, Ethel." Reluctantly she moved.

Roberta preferred this time to clean the rooms: while they were at lunch. She cleared the beds, throwing the lumps of bedding in the cart and making the beds again. Ethel's room was in need of a good cleaning. She couldn't help it with the incontinence, but dang! Ethel had made a mess again. The stuffed monkey and the bedding all needed washing. Roberta cleaned the bath and moved on to the next room. She was making headway today and might get the wing done before everyone came back.

It was a delightful luncheon. Ethel was pleasant. Most of these women were her grandmother's age and she had always been polite to older people. They had given her pudding and apricots today. She secretly wished for apricots every day, yet these weren't as full of flavor as those that had grown in her father's orchard. Oh, what lovely pies and tarts her mother made.

She thanked the ladies she sat with and made conversation about the war. She had not listened to the radio in more than a week. The gentleman at the next table was a Captain, and she asked him if he knew Jim's unit, but he would not speak to her.

Ethel had this vague idea that she must say her thankyous and goodbyes soon and leave. She grew anxious and began to have those bad feelings again. Ethel was too late. Someone took her arm and began leading her away in a direction she did not want to go. This was after lunch and she needed to check on her baby and would like a short nap for herself. She thanked them but said that she would need to check on her baby, and still they urged Ethel off to a chair with the old women and then she saw Uncle Billy and became excited. She waved and threw him a big kiss. This was better, Ethel had no idea that Uncle Billy would be here. Was that Auntie May with him? Ethel wished she had her glasses with her. She did not want to be rude so called out a warm welcome.

The lady was talking on and on. Ethel's mind wandered and she nodded several times. The baby had been a messy eater and there were bits of pudding on her. She was wearing an apron of sorts and was glad for it. Sometimes babies were messy, but they had to be loved. She loved her Tommy. Twice she had tried to excuse herself politely, but the ladies on either side of her were deaf and strapped into big metal contraptions.

She felt sorry for them, but her baby was crying, and she had to get to him. It was her duty to comfort him. "Let Me Go, Tommy is crying." She had said this over and over until finally they helped her up and she headed down the hall.

When Ethel came to the room, she saw her clock. It was time for her nap. First, she checked, but the baby was gone. Ethel was frantic looking for her baby. She screamed and cried. "Tommy, Tommy, Tommy," but when the nurse arrived, they told her she did not have a baby. She called for her father who was someone they would listen to. He was a powerful man. So, she called for her father but was told he was dead, and she cried. "Your mother and father have been dead for years, Honey."

What, her mother and father were dead? How could that be? Ethel took to her bed and cried all afternoon. Her baby was gone, and her parents were dead. Her man was dead in the war and no one cared or wanted to help. In the middle of the afternoon, she had a drink of water and some pills that helped her sleep.

With the laundry mostly done, the clothing was stacked and taken to the rooms. Ethel's stuffed toys and clothing were put away, and the Afghan folded on the foot of the bed. The monkey was laid there. Within minutes Ethel was rocking Tommy. He had come home. They were safe and happy.

Outside Companion

I like the wind to blow and yawn
Gusting outside my window.
While I, inside, am warm and calm
Wrapped-up beside the fire's glow.

With lamp at hand, I read a book
And visit places far afield.
I sail on ships and search the nook
Where fantasy all my treasures yield.

Moan the night, while I relax upon my bed.
My back and feet are warm.
No other noise disturbs my mind
Though you, might swing the blind.

Horseman

Full bodied contact and you feel the beast beneath you
Stretching and moving, rounded and solid, carrying you.
Excitement and sometimes fear, on that you can bank.
Sweat too, and nothing smells like this grain-fed tank.

The miracle is that you are a living part of it all.
A man-beast with intelligence and purpose dual
in the rhythm of bumping and riding it's a partnership.
Together, but one as you race, sway, falter, and dip.

Have You Seen the Elk Run

On some shaded paths, dark spiritways,
The forest transcends the deep winter....
In dark snowy glades there, elk appear as if by magic, silently.
They are, and then are gone again.

Part of the forest, part of the trees,
The shadows that live and move quietly
like a turning leaf in the darkened trail, like ghosts.
They sense you there and all you hear are the rumbling of hooves as they
flee.

Again, missing the sight of antlers,
There is the steam from their nostrils and
the hot steam from their piss in the snow that
betrays their spectral presence and
tells you they are flesh and bone.

Levelers

Snow is the leveler that hides
Mistakes in gardens far and wide,
Summer blunders no one can tell
When winter casts its blanket spell.

Time is the leveler that abides
To whom all may now confide,
The stupid things each would forget,
All have done, and long regret

Wind Pausing for Breath

The fleet wind that blows ice crystals into my eyes
is the same that flings the clouds across the skies.
I've seen perfectly sunny mornings that end overcast
with high winds that send down the torrents so fast.

Wind howls around my tidy house all night
sometimes shrilly calling to give me a fright,
But I'm buying none of that because I'm safe.
I'm a full bodied, plan ahead man, no little waif.
I like the wind when it drives the dirt devils in the field
and blows the trees, in gusts where ripe apples yield
to the pressure of the breezes and bring a few crashing
in the bright days of Autumn of farmers harvesting.

So whip and blow and gust all day and all night
ordering tumble weeds careening in half flight.
Down valley you speed and tease up the hill
But the time will come when you are worn out and still.

Bumpy Ride

Others crowding, Harold flings the dice across the table. "Seven" makes him the winner. Her tug reminds him not to ride the crest: he flags his money, turns and smiles. A real smile of happiness: he is a winner once more and they will eat. Smart, he hands the money to Mamma, and she will manage it. It may last a few months this time. A dusty road home in an old pick-up makes them reflect about the bumps and twists in life. The bumps bind them more than money in mama's bag.

If

If I had a dog
We'd walk along the shore.
The sandy gravel at our feet
We'd walk and walk some more.

If I were a sea bird
A'crying overhead,
I'd dip and dip and soar
To coast the airway sled,

If I had a true love,
I'd hold him in my arms
Then I'd pray and pray to God
To keep us both from harm.

Wild Eyed Game

Silver flash, I saw the streak across the floor,
And when I looked away once more.
Here pranced Toby 'cross the floor.
With back arched high and tail straight up.
He hunted specters... a game made up.

Young, silver-gray ... Toby likes to run and play,
and often spends the whole long day

in wild excursions with big mice I cannot see.
He cannot lay still: He chases flies.
Though sometimes, he takes naps with me.

I smile inside. I have the upper hand,
a game I know that drives him mad.
Tonight, he will play with a string I hold,
raised upon his hinder paws with claws,
To box like Dempsey with white gloves.

One Down

The sun beat down with temperatures soaring to 123 degrees, maybe higher. Almost platinum, sun-bleached hair, and Jason's skin was deeply tanned.

He envied the lizards and snakes that could crawl into the shadows of rocks. His communications unit provided day and night observations followed by information sharing.

Jason never questioned what the higher- ups did with such information. He assumed it was critical and of some importance somewhere. He'd sworn to protect the communications with his life, as had the others. It was duty.

Drones made getting information delivered faster and easier. Convoys were just sitting ducks, while telecommunications were easily blocked or intercepted, but drones could carry stored data information with less risk. Sweat trickled down the back inside of his shirt.

She was not large or small, an average adult female North African Sand Owl. Her burrow was in the compacted sand, and under the scorched earth was a nest with babies protected from the sun.

Small lizards, snakes and unwary birds fed her chicks. Every night she rose over the sand and headed out at low altitude to hunt.

Jason was sweating profusely and removed his shirt hoping for a desert breeze to momentarily cool his body by the miracle of evaporation. Jason took his turn watching the sand, always the sand.

Sand, sun, and heat were his life. Dazed or trance-like, they trained their eyes to detect even the smallest movement, any change in a shadow or pattern did not get by them. They drank water and ate salt tablets. Food seemed to make Jason lethargic and nauseous. A soldier had to eat, or he'd be carried out sooner rather than later.

All day he took his turns and at one point he day-dreamed that he heard rain.

His last trip home was to say goodbye to his best friend. He and Tyler had plans. As soon as Jason was out, they would be together and never need to be separated again. The day of the funeral service was gray, rainy. Soft, sad drops washed the grass, and stained cheeks betrayed his grief, as the sky cried. For those few minutes they held service, the rain held off: the sun shone on blood red roses. Most cars pulled out, but he watched alone just a little longer in the rain. He'd cried and his heart ached completely for his love.

He remembered when the rain caught them on a camping trip: they stayed inside and made tent love. That was their first time. Childhood friends, teen buds and bros, then lovers always together.

After goodbyes, Jason was back in the desert heat too soon mourning his loss.

Heat didn't bother the drones; if anything, they flew more easily, 10 feet off the ground. Some sainted person sent them hard candies in a return flight last week. They weren't permitted to eat them because they might have been poisoned or carried by an intercepted drone. Maybe it wasn't even their drone…. But Jason knew it was. Someone with a sense of humor painted an eye on each side with glitter nail paints that would be hard to duplicate in the desert.

Like the enemy they dressed in desert gear with head covering as camouflage. A drone would go after dark. The enemy didn't send heat seeking missiles against the tiny drones and they went through unscathed.

Lunch was processed ham with a can of peaches packed in heavy syrup. Jason drank every drop of the sweet liquid. He prepared the drone for its flight. The drones had a compartment for cargo, just slits in the body. First the battery, then the USBs, but anything that went inside had to be light. Jason didn't like flash drives loose, so he bundled them with a rubber band. Grabbing the meat can, a flat plasticized thing, he wiped it out with paper shoving the discs inside. It was a good fit. The battery would take the little bird to its nest where it would be recharged and readied for the flight back.

Maybe with candies. Next time he'd hide them and eat them. The drone was packed, and people were waiting on him. Jason looked around studying the dunes. Enemies were there somewhere, not visible.

The other soldiers and he were targets, and after one more check Jason moved away.

The launching was from a different location last night and would be different every night.

Hopefully, that would make them less predictable, keep the launch and the information it carried safer. They didn't launch from base it would be too easy for someone to see if they used the same spot all the time. They trekked out under starlit skies and an unfortunate bright moon.

They heard the shots first, seeing the little dust puffs where bullets hit the sand. Five of them in a straight line. They dropped and returned fire. The information on those flash drives was the reason they were here. They would sacrifice lives to protect it. One of theirs was shot in the leg.

Damn! Maybe the sniper was a lone scout as there were no more shots. Jason took the bird and let her go on the downward slope, watching until the night swallowed her. Her homing device would let her fly with no vision.

He saw a movement. Night shots were iffy, a waste of ammo, but he thought he had a chance.

What the heck: he pulled the trigger. His buddies at close range were already in place. If he could get this one now, they wouldn't have to spend hours searching. Standing on the side of the dune made him an easy target. He heard the shot. The large shell went through his arm and moved past ribs puncturing his lungs. There were more rounds fired. Theirs or enemy fire, Jason wasn't sure. The moon calmed him, he coughed and tasted blood. There was pain.

Everything seemed new and fresh: Jason was sure he heard rain.

The night hunt ending, she picked-up the scent and followed it. The hawk tracked the meat scent and then the whirring noise. She rode the air artfully, but the drone plowed steadily without wavering in its course. She came out of the night and grabbed it, then held as it faltered in the sky. On the ground she tore at it working to tear open the flap with the meat smells. The little tray fell out and emptied in the sand, but there was nothing to eat. She continued hunting and traded her time for a small snake and rodent. Several large beetles completed her dining: she had food for the chicks.

Several days later wild dogs sniffed at the drone and could make no sense of it. One peed on it marking it as part of the territory as the unblinking glitter eye stared at the moon.

Max (Myron) Dunavan

Max (Myron) Dunavan is a native Kansas writer. Born in Atchison, Kansas, he has lived across the state, and is currently residing in Topeka. His background is in program development and management, disability and brain injury, advocacy, public speaking and human services. He writes essays, short stories, novels, novellas, dribble, and tries his hand at several forms of poetry. He enjoys writing science fiction, romance, vampire, western themes, survival, disaster, and a broader genre of fiction. His work is published in anthologies, newsletters, and periodicals.

Aimee L. Gross

Time Dock

If you hope to get an 'A' in AP History in 2070, you've got to get parental permission for time travel. My mom and dad were good with it, though disappointed I couldn't go to visit JRR Tolkien or be in New Zealand for the filming of their ultimate favorite work: *The Lord of the Rings*.

My name is Samwise Carter. Luckily, I was born after they had tagged our Irish Wolfhound 'Gandalf' and 'Frodo' the Beagle joined the family. Anyway, all student travel back in time in Topeka, Kansas is limited in range and duration. One day, one hundred mile radius.

Our history instructor, Mr. Linnet, makes the arrangements with the commercial time excursion company which has a local Dock. Time Voyages, Inc. provides one 24-hour trip each semester for a teacher and three students to witness an historic event.

The report doc you have to submit afterward is practically a thesis; do well and it can get you into a superior university. That was my goal. I had no particular interest in Carry Nation busting up saloons in 1901, but Mr. Linnet did. As a "Societal Shift of Historical Significance."

After extensive prep, our group entered the Time Dock to be shipped back to Topeka circa 1901. I patted the Failsafe Medallion under my period-correct shirtfront.

Nothing was supposed to go wrong. Everything did.

I came to on my back in an alley, my clothes steaming from the jump effects. Not only did I feel as if I'd collided with a terra-brick wall, I saw no sign of Mr. Linnet or my classmates anywhere.

I heard voices raised in shouts and chanting out in the street. Figuring I'd just slid slightly astray, I sought the rest of my party where the action seemed to be.

I walked into a riot.

Men and women raced in all directions. Police dragged people away toward waiting wagons, clubbing the resistors. I couldn't see well enough, given the chaos, to spot Mr. Linnet, or Lisa and Mike.

Soon, the crowd surged and pushed me along as they fled the scene. I had no choice and could think of nothing but getting away. Maybe I could still sort things out. Was I in the right place? The right time? Why wasn't my

Failsafe pulling me back—they'd never plant student observers in this mess on purpose?

I wandered the Topeka streets until nightfall. A cold wind began to howl and plastered a newspaper against my trouser leg, so I examined it under a streetlamp.

Printed on the correct date in 1901. What had gone wrong?

Hours passed as I wandered, until I spotted a light inside a storefront. I stood, shivering, and stared at the man inside as he tinkered with some sort of mechanical gears. The gold lettering on the window said: Harry E. Gavitt, Medical Devices and Pharmaceuticals.

He looked up at me, just as I passed out.

When I woke, I found myself on a metal cot in his workroom.

"Good morning, son. Are you feeling better?"

"It's morning? Yes, I'm all right. I'd best be going." Speaking with period contemporaries was against the rules, too much risk of altering history. No talk, no touch.

"I'm Harry Gavitt. What's your name?" He extended his hand.

I could see no way to avoid shaking it. "I'm Sam, er, Samuel Carter."

I looked around the workroom, benches and tables strewn with racks and tools, and suddenly remembered a detail from my pre-jump research. "You're an inventor," I said before I could stop myself.

He grinned at me. "Why as a matter of fact, you're correct. Take a look at this." It proved to be an envelope sorting and stuffing machine, which he was clearly proud of.

Gavitt observed me carefully while he described how it worked. It really was interesting, and I asked questions which he answered with an expression of approval.

"Let's take ourselves over to the Harvey House for breakfast. I want to talk to you further." He guided me out the door, my protests notwithstanding.

I might as well break more rules, I thought, because I am starving.

Mr. Gavitt ordered for both of us. Soon the waitress returned and covered the table with platters in a flurry of efficiency. Conversation paused while Mr. Gavitt and I applied ourselves to eggs, toast and grilled fish. Everything tasted so fantastic, I let the need to search for my teacher and friends slip to the back of my mind.

I looked up from the last mouthful of oatmeal (Did people always eat this heartily in 1901?) to find Harry Gavitt regarding me thoughtfully over the rim of a coffee cup.

I swallowed. "Thank you for the meal, sir. You can see, I was certainly hungry."

Mr. Gavitt set his cup in the saucer with a decisive click.

"Tell me about the future, Samuel."

I choked, and then continued to fake-splutter to give myself a chance to come up with an answer. I snatched the linen napkin from my lap and held it to my mouth. How could Mr. Gavitt possibly have figured out about the time travel? Had he seen the medallion––but it just looked like a steel pendant. I frantically raked through everything we had talked about. What did I say? And why would he believe I was anything but crazy if I did slip up, talk in my sleep or something? The waitress approached, looking concerned. I waved her away and took a sip of water.

"Um, why do you ask? I mean, I don't know any more than anybody else. Today. In 1901." I grimaced.

Henry Gavitt pushed his empty plate to the side and leaned forward. "I see in you a vision that is refreshing. Most young people I encounter are drudges, consumed by their day-to-day existence. They don't even try to look ahead, to see how our world can progress. They are stuck, mired if you will, in a present time they don't even wish to change."

From the fanatical glow in Harry Gavitt's eyes, I began to understand the man's passion for inventing. Gavitt's question about the future solicited my prediction, not actual knowledge of what would come to pass. And, I thought, while I can't interfere, that doesn't mean I can't support his vision.

I nodded. "I know what you mean, sir. But look at your envelope-stuffing machine—"

Harry held up a hand and glanced at the other diners. "I don't want to be premature in discussing that publicly, Samuel."

"Sorry. Of course. What I meant to say is, you look into the future every day. People who are looking backwards are going to be left behind, but you won't be. You see the possibilities."

"Possibilities are what make life exciting! I have so many ideas. I need the help of people like you, Samuel, to bring them to fruition. You understood the function of the machine in my workshop at once. Innovation, that's the ticket! Say you want to join me, and you'll have a job and the means to make your mark on the world."

This man's enthusiasm is contagious. He should be more famous than Carry Nation.

"What would I have to do?" I asked. This is crazy, I thought at the same time. How is this going to get me home?

Gavitt beamed like sunshine breaking through storm clouds. "Come back to my workshop and we'll make plans."

An hour later, I sat on a tall metal stool asking myself what I had been thinking at the Harvey House. Gavitt buzzed around the workroom, tossing tins and bottles into what he called a valise. He quizzed me on every product until I felt certain my eyes would be permanently crossed from squinting at the labels. The inventor seemed satisfied at last, if that is what I could surmise from Gavitt closing the valise with a snap. Then, he packed a white shirt and starched collar into a battered leather "train case." He included a straight razor and a bristle brush with a block of soap in a mug, plus some other clothing I thought must be historic underwear.

"You'll have to make do with those trousers, I'm afraid. Mine won't be long enough. And those shoes…Can't be helped. We'll get you to a tailor, first payday without fail. Keep my topcoat. It will be cold where you're going on the lone prairie."

"Wait, what? I'm going?"

"Yes, to Abilene. By rail. You'll deliver these," he hefted the valise, "to my canvassing agent there, old Colonel Corbett, and get some pointers."

"How far is it to Abilene?" If it was 100 miles away from Topeka, the Failsafe would snap me back home to 2070. If the system worked. If it hadn't been destroyed in some freak accident. If the future was still there.

Gavitt pursed his lips. "A distance of 87 miles, I believe. The ticket office will have the exact figure, I'm sure. Why?"

"I…my family, you see. I won't want to be away for too long without explaining about my new job and all."

"Do you need to delay your departure?" Gavitt's expression told me he would be hugely disappointed if the answer was yes. And this was a way to get some miles away from Topeka.

"No, I can go. I just need to let my folks know. Can I…" I searched my memory for the correct term for the period. Not telephone, yet. Few homes had service. "Can I send a wire?"

"To be sure. We'll stop by the telegraph office on the way to the depot."

But, who should I notify, so that it stood a chance of calling attention to my predicament in 1901? If Time Voyager techs were searching for me in 2070, how could I send a distress signal without altering history?

"You'll want something to read on the journey." Gavitt turned to rummage in a desk drawer.

"How long will it take to get to Abilene?"

"Seven hours or so, with the stops. Here, have you read Mark Twain?" He held out a battered copy of _A Connecticut Yankee in King Arthur's Court_.

I nodded. Harry reached back into the drawer.

"Ah, here's one you'll like. *The Time Machine* by H.G. Wells. Only been out a short while. I loved it. Imagine being able to travel through time!"

A knock on the door interrupted our preparations. One of the local druggists, Mr. Milton, arrived to talk to Mr. Gavitt about stocking more of his remedies. My eyes fell on the copy of the newspaper Harry had carried back from the Harvey House. It lay with advertisements uppermost. Help Wanted, For Sale, I skimmed over them. The last section: Personals.

I read these with growing excitement. Techs at Time Voyages, Inc searching for me in 1901 wouldn't only read Carry Nation headlines in the archived newspapers, would they? What if I placed an ad telling them where to find me? Something the tech operator from 2070 would understand but which wouldn't give anything away to the people of 1901 and mess with history.

I checked the masthead for the address of the newspaper office. Not far.

I started composing in my head.

"Mr. Gavitt, would it save time if I went over to send my wire, while you finish your business here?"

"Yes, actually. Then we can drive to the depot. The telegraph office is only a couple of blocks over. Do you know it?"

"Yes," I lied. "But I'm afraid I haven't any money. Could I get an advance on my salary? I hate to ask after all you've done…"

"Think nothing of it." Harry reached into his pocket and passed me a handful of coins. "Should cover your message, plus enough left for sundries on the train."

He turned back to the druggist but swung toward me again. "Oh, wait. I'll send a wire to the colonel, so he knows to expect you." He dashed off a message on a scrap of paper and handed it to me. "Send this along with yours. Milton and I will finish our arrangements by the time you return."

I pulled the overcoat on, thinking, if I do have to stay in 1901, I could sure do worse than having Harry Gavitt for a boss. He's a great guy.

After a brisk walk to the newspaper office, I stood in front of a scratched, dented wooden desk. The bored gentleman seated there chewing on a stub of cigar paused long enough to push a pencil and piece of paper to me with an ink-stained finger.

"Write what you want it to say, an' I'll count the words. Spaces count, too, mind."

Presses clattered on the background as I carefully printed: **Samwise C. via train 87 mi. west. Plan go 14 more in hope of snap. Alone. No others, not even Bilbo Baggins.** The last was for my parents, who would surely be searching for me, too. *The Lord of the Rings* reference would hopefully catch someone's eye.

I handed the paper back to the man.

"You're sure this is what you want to say, boy?" He didn't look at me, ticking off the letters as he spoke.

"Yes. How much to print it daily for a week?"

Though he raised an eyebrow, he only said, "Twenty-eight cents. Pay now."

I'd never counted cash in 2070; no one used it anymore. I didn't know the value of each coin, so I pulled a handful out of my pocket and said, "I'm not from around here. Can you take what it costs, please?"

The man grunted and plucked three silver coins and three copper ones from my hand.

I thanked him and sped toward the door, but then thought to ask, "Can you direct me to the telegraph office?"

It wasn't far. I sent the telegram and returned to Harry Gavitt's place in time to see Milton the druggist exiting. He lifted his hat to me and said, "Good luck on your trip," as he strode away.

Harry clapped me on the back as soon as I walked in. "Ready to begin your adventure, Samuel? The future awaits!"

Let's hope so, I thought. I picked up the valise and train case. We headed to the train station, where I pored over the Kansas map on the wall as I waited to board.

I memorized the area that the map legend designated as 14 miles farther west from Abilene. I'd get to the right place even if I had to walk. While I truly hated to disappear on Mr. Gavitt, it was time to go home.

Breaking News: One of the missing student time travelers has returned today. Time Voyages, Inc. issued a statement reporting the safe return via Failsafe Mechanism and declined further comment. The teacher and two other students remain unaccounted for after the incident. Updates as they become available.

Aimee L. Gross Bio

Local author **Aimee L. Gross** began writing in childhood, as soon as she discovered ink on paper could create magic. She has several novels for Middle Grade and Young Adult readers in the works: *Seven Ways to Break A Curse*, *The Alchemist's Lawn Boy*, and *Jacques and the Pig Spell*. The first two novels in the *Mage of Merced* trilogy, *If Crows Know Best* and *No Mercy From Crows*, are now available on Amazon. Reader reviews have thrilled the author as well as the crows she feeds daily in her backyard.

Readers can find her on Facebook as *Aimee L. Gross, author & artist*. Connect on Twitter *@Aimee_SanG*, or send a message to *agross9999author. com*. Ask her how to tell when a crow is thrilled.

Duane L. Herrmann

Dreamtime World

Jumba took the drawings he made for a hanging house to bed with him. He didn't want to crush them but wanted to use them in his dream. Sometimes he could take things with him, sometimes not, and sometimes things were already there that he needed but hadn't realized. He didn't understand the engineering behind, or above, a hanging house, but he liked being in them. Now he had a floor plan he liked and hoped that was enough. Soon, he was off to sleep.

In the dream, he found himself in long, heavy pants that made walking difficult and a gauzy shirt. Clothing in a dream was always a surprise. He liked the shirt, but the bottom of the pants legs dragged out behind him and he kept stepping on the front of the pants legs. They were, clearly, way too long.

'I don't like these,' he thought and immediately he was naked. That wasn't a problem. Clothes in the dream world weren't the problem that they were when awake. He could walk more easily now and that was what he wanted. And, there in his hands, were the plans. Great!

He remembered the gently, comfortable swaying of the hanging house he'd been in the last time. But, you didn't have bones in the Dreamtime, so it was something else Jumba didn't understand, but just accepted. Dream Time was so different from wake time, one simply accepted and continued.

He had several friends in Dreamtime, some had hanging houses, some did not. One lived in a cave, but she wasn't a Hobbit, not exactly. But the cave was cozy, with a window on each side of the door and a hearth in back with a fire that didn't need a chimney. The fire made no smoke. It was in Dreamtime after all. Things were different there.

But, now he had to pee. He saw a post up ahead that was just above knee height with an angled top. He'd seen them before in previous dreams and knew just what they were for. When he approached it, he looked down and what he saw confirmed his expectation. The center was hollow with a grill just below the surface. There was some detritus on the grill, but as he looked the grill became red and some of the debris dissolved. Trash problem solved. He waited for the red to fade, then peed into the Pee Post. Relieved, he resumed walking.

Off to the side, he saw a distortion in the air, like ripples in glass. He could see space between them, like a knot on the trunk of a tree. He knew that was a Snuggle Nook and climbed inside. The distortion hid him from view and let him rest. He didn't understand the engineering for that either. When he woke up he was in bed, back in the waking world.

"Damn!" He said as he realized which world he was in. "I didn't get much done in that dream!" He got ready for work and wondered why that Dreamtime was so short. 'Maybe I slept a long time there. I guess I REALLY needed some rest if I slept in both worlds.' He looked forward to the night when he could return to the Dreamtime.

Back in Dreamtime, Jumba discovered that the plans he had brought from the waking world were still in Dreamtime and he set out to use them He found someone with knowledge of the engineering of the hanging houses, then found the site he'd had in mind. It was a place he'd been to often in Dreamtime. He had returned again and again. It was a slight hill overlooking a lake with a forest on the other side and snowcapped mountains behind. He didn't know if anyone else might be there, at least he didn't see them. He had learned that, in Dreamtime, it was often possible for more than one person to be in the same place, but not visible to others who were also there. It was sort of like multiple people occupying the same physical place, but at different times. One didn't have a sense of time passing in Dreamtime, but there was a kind of time here too.

The house was finished before Jumba left Dreamtime for the waking world, so he could enjoy it, but only briefly.

'Well, at least I got something done that night,' Jumba thought with satisfaction as he woke up and began to prepare for another day. The day turned out to be rough. It was as bad as any nightmare he'd had in Dreamtime. He knew that he might relive the nightmare when he returned to Dreamtime, but he also knew that the reliving would bring understanding and insights into the experience. Dreamtime was a balance to waking time.

Sure enough, that night, in Dreamtime, he did experience the conflicts of the day, but only in symbolic form which went past the details into the deeper meaning of the events. He understood more clearly how his role had contributed to the trauma, not that he could have changed anything, but he had a better understanding and could move beyond it. And, be aware next time a similar situation began to unfold!

His next day at his job in the waking world went much more smoothly.

That night, in Dreamtime, he saw his Granma. She'd been dead for a decade or more. He was excited to see her! She was the special person in his childhood, and he greatly missed her when she died.

"I've been very busy here," she told him as she enveloped him in the cloud of her love. "In life, I learned how to help people. I'm able to do that here, which is why you've not been able to see me, but now I help them in their dreams. Sometimes they can listen and sometimes they cannot. But, it's much more satisfying than when I was alive."

Jumba didn't quite understand, but he knew understanding would come. He was simply glad to be with her and was thankful for that. He woke up refreshed and encouraged from that Dreamtime. He began to wonder what he might be doing after he died. He resolved to work on practicing his positive, spiritual qualities so that, when he died, he would be able to be more functional in Dreamtime than he was now.

Was Dreamtime really the next world, the next stage of life, after life in the Waking World? Jumba didn't know but was curious to find out.

Grandmother And The Fire

My grandmother, with an unconventional, independent spirit, didn't really care what the rest of the world thought. If you went to her house, and she was washing dishes, she might well ask you to help wash them while she went off to do some other task (she really didn't like housework). A grandchild, or any other relative, was a convenient substitute. When you put your hands into the dishwater to retrieve the dishcloth, which we called a dishrag, you would find that it truly was a rag; most likely a piece of clothing that she had stopped wearing. One "dishrag" I pulled from the water when I was a boy was obviously the remains of a long-used pair of her panties!

I dropped that like red-hot coals!

After my grandfather retired from his office job of forty years, he took a part time sales job just for something to do (he already had eighty acres of land, several out-buildings around the house, chickens and a large garden—we really think he just wanted to be able to drive away alone!). One evening when I was there (a convenient labor force, remember?), his sales manager stopped in for some reason.

The main entrance to the house was the kitchen door (there was no path or sidewalk to the never-used front door). The kitchen was, as usual, a mess. The kitchen table, where Granpa was eating, and counters were piled high with papers, canned goods and some dirty dishes (I was washing others) and miscellaneous "stuff."

After I opened the door to let the visitor in, and Granpa cleared off a kitchen chair so his guest could sit down, Granpa began to apologize for the mess.

"It's not always like this..."

"Oh, yes it is!" Granma declared emphatically as she walked in to see who had come into the house. "This is the way it is all the time." She walked past the guest, took some canned goods off the table, and began to put them away.

The sales manager had no choice but to begin his meeting with Granpa, he didn't want to take a man away from his supper, and he had more to do that evening. It may have been one of the most unusual business meetings he'd ever conducted.

My grandmother did not have an example of motherhood for very much of her life. She was the first to be born in the family and, at that time, her family then lived (others have verified this) in a dirt-floored log cabin in Indian Territory near a native trail. She remembered seeing the defeated natives walk past the house.

A sister was born two years after her.

When my grandmother was eight, she and her sister became seriously ill. They passed in and out of delirium and slept. When they woke up they learned that their mother *had also* gotten sick and died. Her mother's father came from Holton, Kansas, to take her body back home to be buried. My granma was too sick to travel with the others; she was left "with a trained nurse." She was doubly deserted, first by her mother dying, then her father and sister leaving her with a stranger.

My grandmother never fully recovered. She was depressed the rest of her life.

After their mother's death, their father's sisters persuaded him to return to Kansas, where the rest of the family lived, because they were sure he couldn't raise the girls alone. He did and the sisters preceded to divide the family up, one sister to one family, the other to another and the father to a third who needed help with their farm. The youngest sister was considered cute and was pampered, my grandmother was not. She was older and expected to work for these strangers; she resented everything.

My grandmother naturally became defiant and developed a passive aggressive manner of responding. People came to regard her behavior as bizarre long before I was born. I didn't know how odd her behavior truly was.

After my grandfather died, I'd left home for college, but my younger siblings were still at home. In this time the county government decided, for protection of the expanding urban sprawl, that private burning could no longer be done without a permit. Those of us who had lived here for generations found this outrageous, yet we were powerless to alter the decision.

My grandmother, as everyone else in the neighborhood, had been burning her paper trash all of her life (food scraps went to the animals, glass and tin into the gully behind the house – none of us had "garbage"). She had no intention to stop burning her trash now. To pay for someone to haul it away was ridiculous. But she had also heard that some new residents (part of the urban sprawl) had once reported a long-time neighbor who had burned his trash as he was used to doing. She was outraged by this injustice. She was going to burn her trash! By God, she was!!

So, she worked out a plan.

The new resident had seen the burning, so was able to report it. If she burned her trash in a place where no one could see it burning, no one could report it.

Where could she burn that would be out of sight?

Burning in the barn or chicken house was too dangerous, she didn't want to set the buildings on fire. She was not stupid.

She could burn in the empty silo, no one could see inside there, but the window-like openings were awkward to get in and out and pulling the trash through would be even more awkward.

The boxcar! That was ideal.

The boxcar had been obtained by the former owner of the farm. It was new enough that it was all steel (the *older* boxcar at my other grandparent's farm was all wood). The wheels had not come with it, so it sat on the ground. The floor had been detached and used as a bridge over the creek (this was the reason for the purchase), so it truly sat on the ground with a dirt floor. The dirt floor had appealed to my grandmother when they first moved to the farm. That floor and the size of the boxcar brought back vague, faint memories of a time when life was good, when her mother was still alive and she was loved. Granma would sometimes walk inside the boxcar on the dirt floor and return as close as she could to the time when her life was happy and the world was "right." Her early, happy years had been spent in a dirt floored cabin.

The boxcar was perfect. And, being steel, with a dirt floor, it wouldn't burn. There was no danger.

She rolled the empty trash burning barrel into the boxcar. Then brought out the paper trash and dumped it inside and lit the fire. She enjoyed her ability to outsmart the authorities and urban neighbors.

But she had forgotten one little detail that had never been important before: the smoke.

A new neighbor saw smoke coming from "a building" and vigilantly called the fire department!

A short time later my younger brother was driving home past Granma's and couldn't help but see a fire truck in her yard with its lights revolving, lots of cars and trucks that weren't normally there, and a crowd of people. He pulled in too.

He parked out of the way and walked to the crowd of people. Neighbors recognized him and the crowd opened so he could walk to where loud voices were heard. One of the voices was Granma's. When he reached the inside of the crowd, he saw our grandmother facing several fire fighters and shrieking.

"Go ahead! Arrest me!" She cried as she held out her hands to be cuffed. "Arrest an old woman for burning her trash! Arrest me for burning an old newspaper! Go ahead, arrest me! What can I do to you?! I'm just an old woman! Go ahead! Arrest me! Put me in jail! See how people will react to that! They know me! They're my friends! They know I'm not doing any harm, just an old woman burning her trash! A great big man like you comes along to drag me to jail! Well, I'm ready to go! I haven't got much, but I've got my pride! Just take me now and get it over with!"

My brother said he wanted to crawl into the dirt.

The fire fighters stood in stunned silence looking at her.

The neighbors were highly entertained. This is one story they could tell and re-tell for years! It was better than anything that had happened in a long, long time!

In desperation, the fire fighter in front of her grabbed her wrists. Instantly she stopped. The sudden silence surprised everyone. She hung her head in abject defeat. It was over.

"Ma'am." He said gently to her. "We're not going to arrest you. We're not even going to fine you, even though we should. We won't even write this up. As far as I'm concerned it never happened. Just don't burn your trash in that building any more. Is that clear?"

Granma turned her eyes up to look at him from her downcast face. She had enjoyed the attention and her righteous indignation. This was more excitement than she'd had since Granpa died. And so many people came to see her! The fireman seemed to be waiting for a response, so she nodded subtly.

"Come on, boys." The fireman called to his crew. "Let's go back to the station in case there's a real fire somewhere." The crew rolled up the hoses, returned to their truck and slowly backed out of the yard. The crowd of people broke into little groups to share their own version of events, it was quickly passing into neighborhood myth. Some spoke to Granma, some sympathized with my brother. Gradually people began to leave.

"Well, I showed them a thing or two," my brother heard Granma exclaim as he left. "I can still burn my trash. Next time I'll wait until it's <u>dark</u>!"

He just shook his head as he drove away.

This Year's Letter

Rafiq Alvarez was anxious. Every year, every spring, he became this way. He was eager to read this year's letter. The letters were to members of a community he belonged to. The letter would give an assessment of the progress of the past year. Sometimes it would lay out intentions and plans for the next several years. Once in a while the letter would summarize achievements of the whole international community for the past several years. Those were bonus letters. Rafiq would be so anxious to read the new letter, that a month or so before it would come, he would go back and read letters from former years.

Once, when he was building the house while his young family was living in it, the Letter came in the mail. He had been hoping for it. Immediately after opening the envelope, he sank to the floor, his back against an unfinished wall, and began to read: "Dearly Loved Friends..." That year, at that moment, that greeting pierced his heart with a personal meaning and he burst into tears.

He marveled at that through the outpouring of emotion. He knew he was under stress, but thought he was managing it well. The tears were evidence otherwise. The work on the house was going poorly. Relationships with significant people around him had taken on a sour note. He hadn't realized how much effort it took him just to make it through each day. This statement of love broke through his defenses and he wept. He felt loved.

Duane L. Herrmann Bio

Duane L. Herrmann, a reluctant carbon-based life-form, was surprised to find himself in 1951 on a farm in Kansas. He's still trying to make sense of that but has grown fond of grass waving under wind, trees and moonlight. He aspires to be a hermit, but would miss his children, grandchildren and a few friends. He is known to carry baby kittens in his mouth, pet snakes, and converse with owls, but is careful not to anger them! His full-length collections of poetry include: *Prairies of Possibilities, Ichnographical:173, Family Plowing, Remnants of a Life, No Known Address, Praise the King of Glory,* and *Gedichte aus Prairies of Possibilities, Zephyrs of the Heart,* plus a science fiction novel: *Escape From Earth,* and a number of chapbooks.

Individual work has been published in more than a dozen anthologies and *Midwest Quarterly, Little Balkans Review, Flint Hills Review, Orison, Inscape, Lily Literary Journal, Hawai'i Review* and others in print and online in English and several other languages he can't read. He is the recipient of the Robert Hayden Poetry Fellowship 1989, and the Ferguson Kansas History Book Award 2007. He survived a traumatic, abusive childhood embellished with dyslexia, ADHD (both unknown at the time), cyclothymia, now PTSD.

Duane Johnson

Instant with Compassion's Eye

Their argument has bled upon my face
a stain too deep for photographs to capture.
The pain endured by free men buried here,
the pain of loved ones living
now, without them
burrows like a bullet in my brain.

Yet, there he poses by his camera,
enjoying banners, brass and pomp,
unaware of how this battle haunts me,
for here on Cemetery Hill lurk
specters of my mistakes.

While our servitude to "principle"
has split the law in two,
pride and passion kindle prejudice, burning
schism's trail from sea to blue-gray sea.
Now, this grim day after, we commemorate,
with stones, the poisoned fruit of ideology.

This solemn rite inaugurates
the most urgent challenge I shall ever face:
love's weary work of binding wounds.
And he would forever
make me still.

I'll not be still for black, hollow boxes
or for black, hollow minds
that scheme to make a pageantry of fratricide.
Those who wish for visions of my pledge
must catch me in an instant with compassion's eye,
for reconciliation cannot wait
for idle photographs.

Tightening the Seam

It just felt like something was going to happen.
Maybe the way aspen leaves barely quivered
and how the alpenglow recast its golden hue upon the stage.
Certainly there was something in Jerry's voice on "Ripple"

as the crowd, now quiet, leaned toward him.
It's then that I felt them stir in both brain and breast:
those mystic threads of intimacy
drawing everyone closer, tightening the seam.

It's happened countless times in life,
beginning with an intimation that we'd better pay attention
or miss some blessed event.
Cues and outcomes are never the same,

but the stirring of those threads through brain and breast
always tweaks our senses just before the moments tighten
and as every soul around us draws closer to the seam
we can see in their eyes they feel it, too.

Timbered Choir

Today his timbered choir sings, bird songs
weaving his words with silence, in rhythm
with leaves. It's Sabbath of course; no church bells
invade this river-edged wood. In red soil
of his Bluegrass farm, his tiller is still
today. Barn doors are closed, and he's strolling
in quiet relief from six days of toil.

This holy day will bow to Labor Day,
an extra respite paid to those who sweat.
I wonder what he'll do to honor time;
meanwhile, he has pad and pen to serve him
until the sun goes down. What to record?
What metaphors and rhymes might incubate?
What lyric will his timbered choir sing?

Immersed in sacred service through his verse,
he keys his voice above the timber's crowns
in harmony with spirits of the soil
then channels earth and heaven with his themes.
Disciples in his woodland chuppah's shade
vow to wed their future to creation
while living light streams through the canopy.

Somewhere in the Water

For you, fishing is a science.
For me, it's art.

Perhaps that's why I catch fewer fish,
but I resist fishing by the numbers
because I mimic awkwardly.

True, sometimes I cast from pool to riprap
like any logical angler
and feel unseen tugs in the water,
same as you.
Like you, I bend the rod to pry
my hidden prize from the depths,
resisting its lure to meet halfway
and endure its baptism.

Still, my cast, while rippling shallows
you'd know better than to visit,
curls from my left hand with graceful arc,
bearing my signature,
and I know you wouldn't have me change it
for convenience's sake
—to catch more fish,
to feed the multitudes,
to bring abundance to the market,
or even to save the whales.

Floating flies and wading boundaries
has become my favorite pursuit. The art of fishing
explores shorelines nature mandates
then bends them to allow each cast
that doesn't harm the water.

When art and science meet, lines tangle.
At any moment, I expect your unseen
tug, resisting,
trying to reel me toward you.
It will take courage for both of us
to meet half-way,
somewhere in the water.

In the Falling Snow

It's the chicken-or-egg dilemma.

I pondered this most recently on Sunday
when, while fishing for distraction
from a cancerous prognosis, it began to snow.
Flakes meandered down until they melted
in the river to begin another cycle.

Or, does the cycle end with river flowing
so that the circle recircles when
water turns to vapor?
Or, is the final segue vapor rising?

These thoughts were still revolving when
the start of darkness sent me home to sleep.
Then dawn on Monday woke me with
the answer, which I immediately forgot, so now,
once more, I'm in the dark about which phase
is the start. But regardless of what works
I do or fail to do six months to a year from today

this simple fact, at least, I know:
my faith is in the falling snow
whether it bring ending or
beginning.

Mountain Climber

He climbed too close to sacred peaks.

On Sundays we would shake our heads
and let him know how mad it was
to scale edges. Once we heard
him joke about a scarcity
of air at rarer altitudes.
And several times we watched him pray
while dangling from a precipice.

So, no one feigned surprise that day
Emanuel collapsed near one
such sacred peak. But dying slowly
gave him time to find his voice
and reminisce about grand vistas
none of us had ever seen
while trailing lower altitudes.

Our Genius Eyes

Some solution in my soul
cleanses the lens of my Genius eye
whenever I consider a stranger.
Some penetrating agent dissolves
cataracts of contempt
that would cloud my quick perception
of kindred spirits.

In early Cambrian days
our native eyes emerged from dust
with specks embedded,
and in our struggle to survive
seemed best fitted to focus on enemies.

But in this integrating age
we've begun to perceive our greatest struggle
is to evolve from our predator nature
by learning to sustain one another.

And we owe this revelation
to some solution in our souls
that cleanses the lenses of our Genius eyes
until we clearly see
a landscape free
of enemies.

Poet of Cocoons

Poetry, sometimes cocoon,
more often is ointment on a wound
called the human condition.
A fan of cocoons to ease transitions,
my suspicion is too much focus on the wound
leads to spiritual malnutrition.
So when I write, I spin cocoons
with a butterfly's ambition.

Some need salve to soothe the wound, I don't deny,
but if your embryonic spirit wants a loom
to weave a womb where it can lie
until you're ready for the sky
here am I, poet of cocoons
and midwife to your butterfly.

Golden Age

We've dreamed it since the sons of Solomon
claimed to glimpse it in the setting sun,
promises of a Son that sets the world aright
with us in charge.

We pretend it's not about politics,
convincing ourselves it's about being right
enough, to stay in charge.

It's right around the corner, this golden age,
through the wormhole by-passing any moral code of conduct
that could slow us down.

But in brief moments of sanity, we know
such thinking will only slow us until it ends us.

In these random, lucid moments
(becoming more frequent, by the way),
we're learning not to get sucked into wormholes,
learning to pay closer attention to the Spirit
that can lead us back to the Golden Code,
the Spirit that strengthens us as we struggle to live its code,
then purges and purifies our souls in Its Fountain of Grace.

Still, pure self-interest tries to punch the clock
on Monday, 9 a.m., and not punch out until Friday, late.
In between, we toil for our wealth,
wealth flowing from hard, honest labor,
and no free lunch, thank you very much!

But our auras shine through our fig leaves,
and my undeceived soul sees what my intellect would deny
that being born white, male, and straight in my neighborhood
is the biggest free lunch of all,
and every neighborhood doles out some free lunches.

So with a prayer and in company of angels, we're called
to set our Captain's compasses toward Spirit's mystic source
neither knowing nor caring when we might arrive,
never letting wind nor wave deter our golden intentions
lest gold dust prick our eyes along the way.

Because the Golden Age will come when golden thoughts
eclipse our thoughts of gold,
when we toss aside idols of metal and stone
and lay our baser selves upon the altar;

when we daily spread Thanksgiving bread
for those too hungry to savor, too thirsty to yearn,
until they have strength to savor and yearn;

and when we grant permission for ten thousand subtle courtesies
to transform and tame our truly liberated wills;
then together will we tap into ourselves and each other
to usher in the Golden Age.

Until then, our best course is to keep steady keel
sailing toward Salvington through rough Seas of Transition
while our guardians of faith embrace us
and the vanguard of progress exhort us and teach us,
and wish us all Godspeed.

Duane Johnson Bio

Duane Johnson is a retired journalist, who now primarily writes poetry. He is also a former state president of Kansas Authors Club. He has published one volume of poetry, *Evolution's Promise,* and is working on two other volumes of poetry. He also has published a novel, *Herald of the Resurrection.* He was Kansas Authors Club Poet of the Year in 2022. He lives in Topeka, Kansas, and is married to a social worker. They have two grown children. He lives in a modest house with gray siding on a dead-end street with a chain saw, fishing gear and kayak in the garage. The near-by four hundred-acre lake is his laboratory.

Ruth Maus

Scar

In the little curio shop located deep
in The Valley of Pain, a holy place
peddling odd icons and alternate
realities,
you picked up the scar and brought it home.

From that day on you and your scar were
inseparable.
You filtered life through the young scar,
bent to its demands, protected it from
all things inflammatory. You wore it

like a combat medal pinned
on skin
and psyche, the graffiti
of biology, the logo of survival.
One day when your mind was clear

you inhaled beyond _I am wounded_—
the scar you had labeled unlovely
had infused you its effortless glitter,
waiting for you to recognize
it had been a star all along.

Hard Pan, Daffodils

There came a time when we needed spring, when
the mud mush slops and bitter blasts pitted the
voltage of longing against the fuse of endurance.
Nobody seemed clever anymore. We
needed laughter, but how does one demand
funny? Always the Sir Authorities, cranky
about mental health, telling us what by now
our penitent brains had already ossified:
that when sorrow contorts our freckled journey
there is no savor, only the leavings.

Homage

I made the graveyard pilgrimage to see
the old New England plot, the grave of Emily.
An iron fence around the stone held sway
in keeping all admirers away,
but didn't stop ecstatic "Wild Nights" quotes
or scribbled praises left on many grass-stained notes.

I was a young girl then and quite obsessed,
so went there hoping my verse could be judged and blessed.
As if her simple greatness could be found
and passed from some cold oracle in the ground,
to lend my work her authenticity
and stroke the hopeful feathers of my vanity.

But the Belle of Amherst held her secrets dear
and spoke no word of her instructions in my ear.
She was to such requests as mine immune,
consigned to Immortality that afternoon.
I left the grave and never went again,
although I still write poems every now and then.

1985 and 09-28-18

Ruth Maus Bio

Ruth Maus of Topeka, Kansas, is the author of poetry books *Valentine* (Meadowlark Books, 2019), a Finalist for the 2019 Birdy Award; and *Puzzled* (Meadowlark Books, 2022). Her poems have appeared in *Inscape, Grecourt Review, River City Poetry, The Orchards Poetry Journal*, and *Lighten Up Online*. She represented Smith College at the annual Glasscock Intercollegiate Poetry Contest. She is a former newspaper and magazine columnist and corporate communications executive.

James Para-Cremer

Butterscotch

There's a butterscotch *on your dresser*
Left there months ago
Bottles of perfume collecting dust
Next to the half dead candles
I don't know why I noticed
These things today
Something inside me woke up and noticed
The keepsakes of our love

Clothes on the floor
Dresser drawers are open
Spare change in a mug
Who's to say
That dried roses 'round your mirror
Won't be dearer to my heart
Anything can happen when you're away

[Pre Chorus]
Perhaps these things just keep me from feeling blue
Feeling blue from missing you
If you could would ya, would ya choose to be?
Here with me... here with me…

[Chorus]
Aww things could be nice
Here with me
Awww things could be nice
    Here with me
      Awww it would be nice
      We'd get nothing done
      But that's half the fun

Of lying around the house
Lying 'round the house...
Lying 'round the house...

Sunlight breaking through the frost
And onto our bedroom floor
I can still see the pins you wore
When you tore your dress on the plaza

[Pre-Chorus]
[Chorus]

Alone

Sometimes alone I sit at home and listen to the wind blow
It speaks to me of memories that I hold dear
It was only yesterday that you went away you're no longer here
And I feel the need with the coming rains to have you near

Gazing through my window screen and out into the street
Nothing moves... no children play... in the summer's heat
And the wind is blowing back my curtain... reminding me of the times
Lying on white linens remembering when you were mine

Your days float by questioning why of those who came before
Song birds sing the songs of love, but yours are filled with sorrow
And you come to me on your knees begging me to set you free
But after all it was you who left me

[Outro]
But after all it was you
But after all it was you
But after all it was you... who left me
But after all it was you who left me

Saucers in the Sky

Johnny sees saucers in the sky some nights
Everyone nods politely knowing he's a bit off time
Sue, she sees little veggie green men
Wandering through the streets at night
Everyone nods politely
Not wanting to seem unkind

    [Chorus]
    But what have you seen?
    Just between you and me
    Did you find the secrets of Loch Ness?
    Come on baby please don't make me guess

Freddie's stocking up on bullets and canned Spam
No one wants to listen to his treatise on Mein Kampf
Janey dresses down to hide the wealth of her birth
Everyone tries to ignore those creases in her shirts

    [Chorus]

And children are getting shot on the streets and in their schools
But everyone needs their guns for protection from "Amir"
Neighbors shutter their windows, locking their doors and gates
Watching their TVs and learning lessons of hate.

    [Bridge]
    Our thoughts and prayers go out to you
    There's nothing more we choose to do
    We ignore and accept the oddest things
    Telling ourselves we can do nothing

    [Chorus]

Simply Simple

Mother doesn't call to check on you, like the way she used to do
And your family albums portray those memories you wish viewed
Your Polaroid skeletons are disposed of easily
While you sit drinking your designer coffee.

Passing time listening from your corner booth.
Picking up on the idle gossip in the afternoon.
Tuning into what is said casually in a crowd
Tuning into what is whispered as the noise dies down.

[Chorus]
Their lives seem simply simple as you watch the crowds go by
Staring through that pane of glass that separates all those lives.

My friends keep asking me, they don't ever see
The friend in you that you are to me.
And I've begun to wonder if you're the kind of friend
That'll keep all my secrets locked up in a little tin.

[Chorus]
Your life seems simply simple as I watch you walk on by
Staring through that pane of glass that separates both our lives.
 My life is simply simple as I watch the world go by
Staring at that pane of glass reflecting back my eyes.

Daughter

When we first heard of you
My darling you
Held our hearts
A dream come true from out of the blue a wish on a shooting star

Now patience never was
A virtue I had much of
But wait, is just what I'll do

Months have passed
The seasons changed
As we wait for you
We've busied ourselves making ready your room

And though we haven't yet met
Your mother and I agree
There's room enough in this family for three

Snowman Family

(James Para-Cremer and Brett Taylor)

Car trunks slam without goodbyes that's the way they always leave
Stuck inside of Lawrence on another ice blue Christmas Eve
I wish my best dog was still around for a little company
I turn the TV on so it's not just me and my snowman family

Daddy was a cop more girlfriends than he had time
Momma asked him to never bring it home I was the only one that saw her cry
She said "I gotta feel the sunshine on my face", a bunch of strangers adopted me
I'm a product or just a victim of my snowman family

[Chorus]
Darkness hates the light
It exposes all the crimes
If I was ever gonna find my way
The sun would have to shine
When winter was finally over
Standing in the warmth of being free
Heaven is a front yard
Without a snowman family

I only leave the trailer to paint cakes at the ice cream shop
Blue eyes and raven black hair floated 'cross the floor and the world stopped
Cups of coffee 'til dawn in Perkins talking about nothing and everything
When she looked at me I met love, the kind you need to build a family

[Chorus]
Darkness hates the light
It exposes all the crimes
If I was ever gonna find my way
The sun would have to shine
When winter was finally over
Standing in the warmth of being free
Heaven is an Iowa girl
That melts a snowman family

[Outro]
The healing is never over
With each day I get more free
Heaven is a front yard
With a boy and a girl smiling at me

James Para-Cremer Bio

Born in 1971, the eldest son of two AmeriCorps VISTA volunteers assigned to rural Wimauma, Florida, **James Para-Cremer**'s first home was a "renovated chicken coop" made of concrete blocks and corrugated metal sidings. As a child his family moved frequently; eventually relocating to the Midwest. James studied art and music at the Kansas City Art Institute and the University of Kansas where he holds an advanced degree from KU's School of Applied Behavioral Sciences.

James currently resides in Topeka, Kansas, where he frequently ruminates on the topics of love and family and the motivations of the heart—central themes in his writing, art, and music.

Julie Sellers

What's Right

It was 11:00 p.m., and Leon Frank's office door yawned open with a come-hither appeal. Elaine stood frozen at the threshold. She had fantasized about a moment like this, but now that it stared in her face, what would she do?

Go in, Elaine thought, glancing about the empty hallway. See what dirt you can find on the snake. He has to be hiding something; no one keeps their office locked even to go next door to the copier if they're not. Go on; go see what it is.

Elaine took a breath and raised a foot. The floor creaked its disapproval, and she immediately lowered it.

Why is this so hard? she wondered. We don't have security cameras, no one else is working at this unholy hour, and that man is a supervisor straight off the screen of _9 to 5_. Why should I have a conscience?

But Elaine knew the answer. She could still hear her grandmother's voice from her childhood: "Always do what's right."

Darned lot of good that's done me lately, Elaine thought. She plugged her ears to her grandmother's lessons and retraced the litany of Frank's sins as she stood in the space between the light of the hallway and the shadows of his office.

It all started with the cryptic last-minute emails. "Come see me at 8:00," he'd write, leaving her no time to make the designated hour. And then, he berated her for her tardiness.

Then, it progressed to withholding information on projects so she looked the fool in front of the boss.

There were also the veiled threats of putting her on work improvement if she didn't accept extra duties.

But the crowning glory had been the day before when Leon swept into the most important contract of the year and claimed credit for the weeks of work Elaine and her co-workers invested.

"He's so slick about it," Marie grumbled that afternoon at the corner bar.

"Anyone got any rat poison?" Donna asked.

"No, I want poetic justice," Elaine said. "You know, the grand revelation that he's embezzled money or proof of corporate espionage or copyright infringement. Something like that."

"I like the way you think," Marie said, signaling the bartender for another round.

"My grandmother would say, 'you reap what you sow, so always do what's right,'" said Elaine.

Those were the very words that pinned Elaine to the threshold of Leon's office now. She longed to go in and root through his files to find that one piece of evidence to end his reign of terror. But she couldn't budge.

Elaine sighed, popped her earbuds into her ears, and turned from temptation. She stomped down the hall to the elevator as if to emphasize her decision, the volume on her phone raised to drown out any lingering voices calling her to enter. The music was so loud she didn't hear the muffled groans from the floor in his office where Leon Franks lay sprawled behind his desk. The custodian would find him the next morning, dead from a heart attack, incriminating documents fanned out on the floor around him where he'd fallen.

The Mystery at the Salon

"What do you suppose we'll see on TV this evening?" Fred asked as he pulled the silver Buick into the parking lot in the shopping center where Sport Clips was located.

"Looks like Trixie is working," Irene said, methodically removing food from the takeout bag.

"Never a dull moment when Trixie is working," Fred said.

The parking lot had become a part of their weekly routine during the two years of pandemic reality as the elderly couple dutifully practiced social distancing during their weekly trip from their farm into town for curbside grocery pick-up. The large front windows of the walk-in salon for men made for interesting viewing. They didn't really know the stylists, whose names they'd chosen based solely on their observations over the accumulating months, but they filled in the blanks and backstories themselves. Sometimes it was a sitcom and others a drama, and they considered the view their own private weekly show as they ate.

"Here comes Gene," Irene said, nodding towards a gleaming black Cadillac Escalade.

It parked, and a lanky man in his thirties climbed out.

"He and Rosie must've made up," Fred said. He pointed as a stylist of about the same age rushed out to greet Gene with a television-worthy kiss before both returned to the Escalade.

"That's a relief, after the fight they had last week. I was worried it was over."

"Is that Russ in the chair?" asked Fred.

Irene leaned forward, adjusted her trifocals, squinted, and nodded. "That's Russ."

"I've never seen a man get his hair cut that often."

"I still say he's a CEO or VIP or something with letters," Irene said.

"And I say he's interested in Shirley. He always waits till her chair is open." Irene sniffed. "It could be both."

"Or something else altogether," Fred agreed.

"I guess we'll just have to wait and see."

"Who's Trixie working on?" Fred asked.

"I don't think we've ever seen him before."

"Doesn't look like she knows him. She's not talking much," said Fred.

"Suppose he'll be a regular?" said Irene. She opened her bag of chips.

"Let's hold off on naming him until we see him again."

They ate in silence, watching Trixie work and Russ lean on the counter and chat up Shirley as Rosie and Gene made out in the Escalade.

"Kind of a dull episode," Fred said after several minutes.

"Maybe it'll spice up before we leave," Irene said hopefully. "You never know with TV."

Russ left, and Rosie hopped pink-cheeked from Gene's Escalade with a giggle, a blown kiss, and a wave to her leading man. She crossed paths with Trixie's stone-faced client as he exited. Fred and Irene were separating their trash from their recyclables when a black Dodge Charger Hellcat with red detailing roared into the parking lot. Fred and Irene stared as Trixie looked out the window. Recognition registered on her face, and she frowned. The car door opened, and the epitome of a tanned bad boy with windswept auburn hair stepped out in tight-fitting jeans, a T-shirt molded to his sculpted chest, and cowboy boots.

"Now, this is interesting," said Irene.

"Indeed," said Fred as Trixie rushed out the door to greet the newcomer with a frown. Fred hit the button to lower his window and turned up his hearing aid.

"What are you doing here?" Trixie said.

"Dapper Dan there must be an ex-boyfriend," Fred predicted.

"Shh! I can't hear." Irene lowered her window and rested an arm nonchalantly on it as she leaned out.

"I came to see if you want to go get your daily hit," Dan said.

"Hit?" said Irene. "Surely Trixie hasn't been an addict all this time."

"I told you—I need to give that stuff up." Trixie crossed her arms.

"Come on. One little hit won't hurt you." Dan flashed what he knew was an irresistible grin.

"It's an expensive habit. And that much can't be good for you," said Trixie.

"Are you kidding me? It's just once a day. Come on," Dan said, wrapping his muscular arm around Trixie's tiny shoulders and ushering her towards the Hellcat.

"I don't want to. I mean it." Trixie shrugged off his arm.

"We're going," Dan said. He placed both hands on her shoulders and forced her into the waiting car. Fred and Irene sat speechless as Dan slammed the driver's door and raced out of the lot, tires squealing.

"Was Trixie just kidnapped by a drug dealer?" Irene gasped.

"I think she was," Fred said.

"We have to do something." Irene fumbled through her handbag for her Tracfone.

"What are you doing?"

"Calling the police."

"I didn't even get the plates. Did you?"

"No. Here—I can't dial with these nerves." Irene shoved the phone towards Fred.

"I will, but you're telling them what happened. You're more observant." Fred punched in 9-1-1 and handed the phone back.

"We've just witnessed a kidnapping . . . At the Sports Clips by the Panera . . . It was Trixie. Well, I don't know if that's her real name, that's just what we call her. She's a stylist . . . Some young fellow who showed up in a black car . . ."

"A Dodge Charger Hellcat," Fred specified.

"A Hellcat . . . He forced her in it to go get a hit . . . What did he look like? Six feet tall. Slender. Wavy brown hair. Tight clothes."

"You noticed all that?" Fred asked.

Irene ignored him. "Where was I? Right here in my Buick with my husband. We were sitting in the parking lot eating our supper, and we saw the whole thing . . . Thank you, we'll wait." She snapped the phone closed and exhaled.

"Well?"

"They're sending someone. I hope they find her in time," Irene said.

Soon, a cruiser pulled in. Fred and Irene donned their facemasks and stepped out of the Buick. Irene resisted every urge within her to remind the young officer that his facemask would be more effective if it he wore it over his nose and not as a chin bra. Trixie's life was at stake; this was no time to pick a fight with law enforcement.

"You the ones who saw the kidnapping?" the officer asked.

They nodded and launched into an animated description of the crime.

"Officer, you need to interrogate the other stylists. Trixie clearly knew Dan," Irene said.

He was spared an answer by the approaching rumble of a well-tuned engine.

"That's him!" Fred said.

"And Trixie's with him."

The Hellcat pulled past, two sets of eyes looking curiously through the windshield. It parked in front of the salon, and both occupants exited, large coffee cups in hand.

"Everything all right, ma'am?" the officer called.

Trixie and Dan looked at each other.

"It's OK, Honey. If he's forcing you to do something you don't want to do, we're here," Irene called.

"I'll handle it, ma'am," the officer said.

"I'm fine," Trixie said. "Why?"

"We had a report of an alleged kidnapping and drug deal."

Dan and Trixie burst into laughter.

"I told you this would happen if you kept calling my afternoon extra-large mocha a 'hit.'" Trixie said with a playful punch to Dan's arm.

"Mocha?" said Fred.

The officer sighed. "So, no coercion and no drugs?"

"Oh, my brother convinced me to go get a sugar-laden coffee I really don't need, but other than that, no, there was no coercion or drugs," Trixie said.

"I am so embarrassed," Irene said.

"We're really sorry," Fred said, eyes cast downward.

"It's OK. It's good to know there are people who care enough about a stranger to try to help."

"But you're not a stranger, Trixie," Fred said.

Irene cut him off with a sharp elbow to the gut.

"My husband means we've seen you here because we sit in this lot once a week to eat our takeout. We haven't been out much since the pandemic started," Irene said.

"I still appreciate it. My name's Renee, and this is Victor," she said. They shook hands and made introductions as the officer retreated to his patrol car to complete his paperwork.

"We're so sorry for the mistake," Irene said.

"It was a sweet gesture. And if you need a haircut, I'll give you the friends and family discount and even fit you in afterhours, so you don't have to worry about having too many people around."

"That's kind of you," Irene said.

"We have to take care of each other, right? Well, I'd better get back to work."

Fred and Irene climbed sheepishly into their Buick.

"I suppose we'd better find someplace else to watch TV when we come to town now," Irene said.

Fred shook his head. "Are you kidding me? Trixie offered us a discount. Besides, we know the characters on this show. I'm never going anywhere else."

The Unexpected Casualty

The piano had been a sore spot from the moment it arrived in all its pomposity at Erik Larsen's modest home. Now, as the muddy floodwaters of the Cottonwood River seeped under the French doors he'd installed just to get the instrument into the house, Erik rubbed a weary hand over his face. He envisioned all the damage a projectile of that size, born along on the implacable waters, could achieve inside his home. Erik regretted anew letting his wife convince him to keep the monstrosity.

Lois had met Erik at the door that day to tell him of her inheritance from a long-forgotten uncle.

"But you don't play the piano."

"I could learn…" Two big tears welled up in her eyes.

Erik acquiesced; he never could stand to see his wife cry. But, when the delivery arrived, he rued his decision. Erik had envisioned a modest upright that he could slide against the parlor wall, not the behemoth grand that was his fate. "Inheritance!" he'd scoffed to himself. "How about a little cash instead?"

But Lois was elated. They maneuvered the piano into the only space it fit, right in the middle of the living room. Lois polished and buffed it until Erik could see his furrowed brow reflected. She immediately began lessons and dutifully practiced her scales, while he sat of an evening attempting vainly to read his paper. Every sour note—and they were abundant—made his flesh crawl, but he swallowed his words at the look of rapture on his wife's face. The piano was her treasure.

And now, he stood on the steps watching the floodwaters eddying around the colossal interloper he had failed to secure in his haste to take anything of value upstairs after sending Lois to her sister's. The water was still rising, and if he didn't act, the walls, windows, doors, the structure itself—everything could be damaged by that mammoth instrument. Cautiously, Erik waded to the French doors, pried them open, and herded the semi-floating piano across the room. It hesitated for an instant before slipping out into the current. "Good riddance," he said, as he slogged to higher ground and his waiting truck.

Later, someone in a third-story window on Main saw the piano bobbing down the street and photographed the unexpected casualty, thinking it quite the joke. That image of Erik Larsen's desperate act became the face of the '51 flood in Florence, Kansas, circulating across the state and the years.

That night, when he told Lois, her face blanched. "It's gone?"

He felt a stab of guilt. "Yes, but we can get an upright for the parlor." She looked stricken. "It won't be your uncle's, but…"

She shook her head. "You don't understand. It's not just the piano. He left me money, too."

"Money?"

"Five thousand. Cash. I wanted to surprise you when you did the addition to the store. I…" She swallowed. "I hid it in the piano."

Julie Sellers Bio

Julie A. Sellers is the author of *Ann of Sunflower Lane* (Meadowlark Press, 2022) and *Kindred Verse: Poems Inspired by Anne of Green Gables* (Blue Cedar Press, 2021). She was the Kansas Authors Club Prose Writer of the Year (2020, 2022) and the Overall Winner in the Kansas Voices Contests (Poetry—2022, Prose—2017, 2019). Julie lives in Atchison, Kansas.

Anne Spry

My Mother, My Muse

Her lips. I can't stop staring at my mother's lips.

I guess they've been glued shut—in evenly spaced intervals—mathematically spaced intervals. I had no idea that's what happens when a mortician prepares a body for cremation.

My stepfather and I stand in the basement of the mortuary, just outside the embalming room. Mother lies on a cart in the hallway, her body shrouded in a coarse white sheet, with only her head and bare shoulders showing, and I fixate on her chapped lips.

I can see dark spaces between dabs of glue. I'm horrified at myself, but I can't tear my eyes away from those lips that once sang hymns of praise and recited original poetry.

Finally, after an awkward silence in this hallway of death, my gaze moves to the platinum hair, dried from decades of covering the mousy brown she always hated. I reach up to smooth it.

We've been invited down here to say our last good-byes, but we're both just standing silently, awkwardly. What do you say to a body in a basement? To lips and a face and hair that you once knew so well but that suddenly don't look the least bit familiar? Who are you talking to anyway? And for whose benefit?

The woman lying on this sterile cart is not my mother. My mother's words, her paintings, her poetry, her prose, all our plans to go to writer's retreats and shopping trips and do mother-daughter things that we missed in years of my adolescent angst and her search for just the right husband to support four kids and her artistic and creative pursuits… all that is gone now.

Cancer closed her lips, after it ate away insidiously at her bones over the last three years. One day she was 71, climbing on the roof of the house she and my stepfather shared, working like a man, scurrying up and down a ladder and using a nail gun to fasten asphalt shingles to particle board. She was hurrying to finish the job before the neighbors reported them for not getting a city permit to build on a room. A few months later she was going for chemo treatments and trying to find someone to take over her duties as editor of an anthology for the writer's group she belonged to. Now she's lying here in the basement of a funeral home with her lips glued shut.

I lived three hours away and the small-town newspaper I owned made it difficult to be with her in the last days. There was no other family member close by to ease her into those final months. Just hospice volunteers, once the chemo drugs stopped working. I came as often on weekends as possible. Those were wonderful visits. We looked through photo albums, picked out funeral hymns and just sat in comfortable silence in the new sunroom to look at her unfinished paintings and her unfinished memoir.

The easy quiet of those last precious weekends contrasted greatly with the often violent drama of our early history. We wasted so many years keeping each other at arm's length, blaming each other for past errors and omissions.

She had me when she was only 18, then couldn't cope when I was a colicky crybaby for the first eight months. She stopped coping for real when my dad abandoned the family by dying in an accident when I was four, my baby brother was two and she was only 22. A string of moves, failed and abusive relationships followed quickly. Along with three more babies.

By the time I left home for college I had slapped the "dysfunctional" label on our family and given up entirely on the traditional mother-daughter relationship. I soon found my own forever family, marrying the oldest son of a big Catholic family, thinking (incorrectly) that doing so would ensure a functional and happily-ever-after life. Heck, I even found a substitute mother in my new mother-in-law and left my biological mom in the recesses of occasional guilt-induced contact. That is, until my second husband–whose mother he adored but who had died–urged me constantly to call her.

Eventually, a stronger mother-daughter tie emerged. We did go to writer's conferences together. We went on at least one shopping trip together. We got reacquainted as mature adults during a long trip to Texas for my niece's wedding.

We were soon sharing newly discovered gifts and talents. I took piano and organ lessons as an adult. So did Mother. She joined a writer's group in her hometown decades after she had poured out her heart in secretly written poetry and furtively entered essay contests. Just before her diagnosis, when it would no longer cause friction with her insecure fourth husband, she began writing columns for my newspaper. Until her cancer treatments made her too sick to continue.

Mother knew my weeks were ruled by Tuesday night newspaper deadlines. Out of sub-conscious consideration (because she was in a coma at the end) she waited until a Wednesday to make her final exit.

That morning, after a grueling deadline complicated by a computer breakdown, my husband and I sat at breakfast. Bleary-eyed, I was on a second cup of coffee when a door in the basement of our house slammed shut. It was June. The air conditioner was running. There were no windows open down there. It was precisely 8 a.m.

Five minutes later my stepfather called. Mother had passed away at exactly the minute the door had slammed. He reported that her eyes had suddenly opened wide, and with a startled gasp, she left us.

And now here we are, down in this dark space, saying goodbye, or at least pretending to. But I know that good-byes aren't necessary. She isn't gone. And my mother is certainly not inhabiting what's left behind in those chapped, glued-together lips and that dry hair.

I do not say goodbye to my mother's body. That would be a sham, a gesture as empty as her clay house is now. But gradually, almost imperceptibly, I assume the chore of living out her unfinished, unspoken and unwritten projects.

I have a book of her essays and poems to compile and publish. Her cross-stitch quilt is stored in a plastic bag in a closet, only half-embroidered. I should finish that. The music she played on her home organ will now need to relocate to my piano so I can play them in sorrow while she listens from a new dimension.

I know that finishing my mother's words and creative works is the more important goodbye. My acts of love and my duties as a scribe will be and have been repeated perpetually through the ages by other daughters and sons for their own loved ones, and even for the orphans and homeless, and all those with no one to record their slots of time and space. All of us have stories to tell and I now feel a compulsion to encourage the telling. Even as I go about this individual act of story preservation.

As I write something nearly every day, as I dream in the essence of story and breathe out God's inspirations, I know my mother smiles her approval. She smiles from ear-to-ear, from radiant lips no longer glued shut. She has given me her voice, her words, her aspirations and ambitions. She now lives on in me. And I will honor her in the only way I know.

Charcoal Childhood

I bought a box of crayons–the giant one with 96 hues,
seeking a name for what my unfocused eyes scan on those
mid-March mornings following a melted snow.

But the two-dollar child's box wasn't much help,
naming fruits and condiments–mustard, apricot, sunflower,
cinnamon-spice, while sounding nice, weren't quite right.
Neither were Duck-Duck Yellow or Silly Celery.

Still seeking, I unearthed a box of my mother's pastels
searching for something exotic, maybe even a scent
like Burnt Sienna, or perhaps a taste like Cardamom.

As I opened the antique clasps, decades of chalk dust sifted out.
Inside nestled gold ochre, amber and straw. Memories came too.
I inhaled ghosts of turpentine rags, felt sable brushes soft against
my cheek and recalled all the tools Mother used on art she hoped to sell.

I remembered the girl I was at eight, complaining when made to help
drag cattle panels into malls, hinge them to hang paintings in stalls.
Mother wished they would sell and hang on someone else's walls.

I skipped along sidewalks at those art shows, window-shopped,
became bored people watching. Until that day she sat me down
for a $2 portrait. Suddenly I couldn't wait to see my image
come to life under charcoal lines impatient to be me.

Now I look at my lawn and realize it's too late,
because the color I first sought is just a whisper.
Deep in the grass I can see forest and mint
sneaking their way up through shades of March.

On the wall behind me hangs the last painting she completed.
I have no need today to name the precise colors her brush laid
into the ressurrection grass. Nor does it matter that I can't call
out the exact shade of brown on the stone rolled away from the tomb.

Anne Spry Bio

A month after the sudden death of her second husband, **Anne Spry** had a mystical dream that detailed a new business based on capturing personal history for writing a memoir. She had already begun publishing books through CreateSpace for herself and others following a 27-year career as a newspaper publisher and editor. Since the fortuitous dream, Spry and partner Cheri Battrick have developed a DIY memoir kit, and Anne has expanded her book publishing to more than two dozen titles under the Personal Chapters LLC banner. They include children's books, memoir and fiction and a few titles authored by Spry. Anne serves as President of District 1 of Kansas Authors Club and produces an occasional newsletter for that group and another weekly publication for a local Sweet Adeline's group.

She is married to a retired military pilot, and they live on a family acreage south of Topeka where Anne spent her first five years.

Barbara Waterman-Peters

Beau

Beau was unique and that was a fact. Of all the young ones, she had the most quirks. No matter what was happening, Beau found a way to make it difficult or funny, depending on your point of view. And from her mother's point of view, Beau was simply exasperating.

Like the time the whole family, aunts, uncles, cousins, grandparents, and that third cousin twice removed nobody seemed to know, gathered near Broussard, Louisiana to celebrate something or other. Everyone was getting along famously until, in a rare moment of silence, Beau piped up with a question. Oh, it was innocent enough, but by the time arguments had ensued regarding one of the finer points in the still-disputed answer, the huge group was reduced to Beau, her parents and four siblings.

Another event had a more humorous outcome but didn't bear thinking about because it was just too humiliating. Beau's mom would often wonder how she had hatched her but didn't ponder the subject overlong as she had four other offspring to care for.

Now one day a carnival came to Broussard. Magically, by that evening the trucks, pylons, wooden structures, and rolls of canvas had become music, color, bright lights, sequins, laughter, balloons, popcorn, cotton candy, and excitement!

It drew Beau to it like a magnet, attracted and hypnotized her like nothing ever had. She couldn't get enough of it. The family had gone together opening night to see all the sights and stayed until it closed. Beau's parents had hoped this would satisfy everyone's curiosity and be the end of it, but Beau wanted more.

She loved the sparkle of the performers' costumes and the funny faces of the clowns and tried to get very close for a good view. Beau knew her parents would never allow another visit, so she decided on the way home to sneak back as often as she could to observe again all the marvels of this place.

On her second forbidden foray, which had been harder to arrange because her father had been very restless, Beau found her usual vantage point blocked by a large, shadowy figure. She had especially wanted to take another peek at a beautiful, shiny necklace one of the lady acrobats wore each night. It matched the gold sheen of the outfit she wore as the star of the grand finale.

The necklace glistened, catching the spotlights in the big tent. Hanging from its chain was a dazzling stone, almost blinding in its brilliance. Beau thought it was the loveliest thing she had ever seen.

The big man in front of her was very quiet, watching the acrobats taking their bows to enthusiastic applause. Beau noticed when she moved slightly that the man was staring at the small golden lady as she left the center of the ring. Suddenly he ran between two tents and disappeared. Beau thought this was odd, but she knew it was very late, so she left the carnival grounds.

She worried that her absence might be discovered and that she would never be able to come back for a glimpse of the special, shiny object. Lost in her dreams of sparkly things, she didn't hear the shouts and running feet until the thuds of rapid footfalls came at her from the darkness. Eerie sounds of distant voices mixed with the hard breathing of the fleeing person, made Beau aware of possible danger. She quickly hid behind a tree but couldn't resist a glance backward. Her eyes widened as she saw the same man she had been near at the carnival. Gripping something in his hand, he ran by, vanishing once again into the gloom.

The next opportunity for Beau was two nights later. She found her favorite place just as the acrobats filed into the tent and began their routine. The golden lady did not seem as happy as before and her special fire seemed subdued. No necklace adorned her. Beau was sad for her and missed the brightness of the stone as it caught and reflected all the lights. Disappointed, she made her way home, her eyes downcast.

Something glittered faintly among the weeds below, capturing the moonlight. Beau stopped to investigate: a little delay in returning probably wouldn't hurt. As she bent to look at the gleaming item, she recognized it. The necklace! Beau could not believe her luck. Her dream of having such a lovely thing had come true. She snatched it up and hurried home.

As quietly as she could Beau put her coveted prize in a secure place because she sensed that her mother would be dismayed by what she had done. Then she went to sleep.

Time flew by. Beau often found an excuse to visit the secret treasure and to admire its beauty. At first, she went every day, always anticipating her pleasure. Then it was every few days and finally every few weeks, the excuses to go becoming more difficult and bothersome to invent.

One day Beau realized that the necklace had lost its appeal somehow. Surprised, she wondered how such a fantastic dream could have lost its shine. That afternoon and all through the long hours of the night she thought about it. Just as dawn arrived the answer came to her.

Beau's family was together a short while later and her mother mentioned that the carnival was in town once more. Beau only half-listened to the plans to go, her mind full of her own ideas. Beau's mother noted her distraction, speculating on what she could be up to now, but only shrugged.

When the sun began to set that evening, Beau and her brothers and sisters led the way to the fun. It was as wonderful as before: bright lights, music, color, laughter, and excitement.

Inside the tent, Beau eagerly searched for the golden lady, as the performers marched in on the drum roll. She was in the center of the group, waving to the audience, and smiling radiantly, the sparkle in her eyes matched by the one around her neck.

Beau relaxed and adjusted her wing feathers, a very happy crow.

Darkness in Tuscany

My sister and I were to board a plane for an early flight home. The flight was so early, in fact, we had to get up the night before.

My niece planned to remain in Florence. That single decision spared her the wretched experience of learning how totally black life can be. Cautioned not to disturb her, I was forced to grope among various black lumps of clothing in my black suitcase inside an unfamiliar black room. My shoes, black, of course, seemed to have gone missing somewhere in the even deeper gloom under the bed.

Meanwhile, my sister was happily splashing about under the one dim bulb in the bathroom. My sister is herself a dim bulb: she is *cheerful* in the mornings and drinks coffee at *night*! The importance of these issues will become more relevant.

It was my turn in the bathroom.

Florentines must be practical people because they have devised a system whereby one can brush one's teeth, shower, and see to other business simultaneously. In a perfect world, these activities would last approximately the same amount of time; however, this is not a perfect world and at the end of the day—or the very beginning—the shower consumes several extra minutes. Imagine one's surprise if one is not the first user of this convenience! I will not dwell on the somewhat questionable elements of this facet of Italian design principles as they are not the subject of this essay.

After overcoming the odds of being awake, clean, dressed, and packed by 4:00, we quietly made our way down to the dark, empty lobby. Our charming little hotel, booked by my ever-efficient and cheerful sister, apparently did not feature coffee before 8:00.

Facts are hazy at this point, but we were evidently whisked away by a taxi through the deserted streets. I will save my Italian taxi stories for a dissertation on near-death experiences.

Eventually we arrived at the airport. At least we assumed it was the airport: dark windows and an empty parking lot lacked that bustling effect. Shadowy figures bearing suitcases were milling around, lost, and confused. Franz Kafka came to mind. We must have paid the driver and joined the ranks of the other sleepy, disoriented individuals.

It was 4:45. My sister's assurances of coffee at the airport were, in a word, groundless.

Word spread that a bus had been dispatched from some mysterious place to deliver all of us to Pisa. The logic of this development was somewhat difficult to grasp until we were informed that the perfectly good airport in front of which we were currently shivering was closed for a holiday. The exact event being commemorated was never explained. Kafka again.

So, there we stood in the inky black cold, the only light furnished by the glow of a cigarette. Tuscan moonlight is only a myth.

At last headlights appeared on the horizon, giving hope to the doomed. Somewhere in Italy an airport was open, and we were going there. My watch showed an evenly divided face by the murky interior lights of the bus. Darkness still held sway outside.

Three hours had passed. I was very quiet.

My sister's cheerful visage began to display a furrowed brow; she started glancing at me occasionally. The bus hurtled through the stygian gloom.

I said nothing. My sister was watching me intently.

In the time it would have taken me to read the Encyclopedia Britannica twice, we were delivered to the functioning airport at Pisa. The Pisans are either more irreverent or more practical than the Florentines, but by then I had no desire to debate the issue.

We rushed to check in—at least my sister did—I have absolutely no idea of what my role might have been. By this time, probably 9:00, I was catatonic.

My sister was becoming frantic, sensing that my good, if silent, behavior was temporary, because she commented frequently on how good I was being. This was certainly an effort to ensure its continuance. International incidents are not pretty.

I met all these attempts with the grace of a sullen seven-year-old.

Perhaps by now in mortal fear that I would openly exhibit such tacky withdrawal symptoms as the DTs, she left me in the crowded, noisy terminal and set off in search of coffee. No doubt some enterprising Italian had realized the black-market value of caffeine. Unfortunately, she had no contacts in that milieu, but desperation is a powerful incentive. And it *was* after 9:00.

Long after: it was 9:45! I still had no coffee and now no sister. On the brink of panic, I felt my system shutting down and darkness closing in. With what little lucidity I possessed, I began to make resolutions about giving up the nasty brew and reforming. I had hit rock bottom. Addiction is a truly ugly thing.

At 9:57 the Tuscan sun began flooding through the windows! My sister was standing before me, having returned from her gallant quest. In her hand was the Holy Grail, a small white Styrofoam cup with a plastic lid through which a lovely little puff of steam was escaping.

Time

Just a few minutes
Left on the clock
'Til I shower and dress,
Arrange my face,
Think the thoughts
To find my place.

Just a few minutes
By my watch
To grab the baton
In this endless race,
To get somewhere
To draw an ace.

Just a few minutes
Shown on my phone
To write some lines,
Find the words,
Spell and gather
Into poetic herds.

Just a few minutes
Remain of my time

To create a work
Bend it to shape
Make it great—
(BONG, BONG—)

NO!! Wait! I'm not done!
Surely, there's time left
On the clock—look it's not quite
Quarter to done. Even the Doomsday
Clock shows a few minutes
Left.

Let me write another story!
Please one more painting!
I'll make—a memento mori—
To this glory we call
Life. I have more to say!
Just one more day!

Or just a few minutes—
I promise I'll say only good things
All that I know or at least
Try to show, to draw
The best of life—not the strife—
(BONG, BONG, BONG…)

Barbara Waterman-Peters Bio

Barbara Waterman-Peters, (BFA, Washburn University, MFA, Kansas State University, Honorary Doctor of Fine Arts, Washburn University) taught at Washburn and Kansas State Universities as well as for Lassen Community College in California. She has received a Certificate of Recognition for Outstanding Achievement from the State of Kansas and the Monroe Award from the Washburn University Alumni Association. In 2011 she was awarded the ARTY for Distinguished Visual Artist from ARTSConnect in Topeka. Her work has been included in more than 300 solo, group and juried exhibits and is in museum, corporate, and private collections. She is represented by several galleries—Jones in Kansas City, SNW in Manhattan, and Beauchamp in Topeka. She owns STUDIO 831 in the North Topeka Arts & Entertainment District (NOTO).

Waterman-Peters also writes about art and artists for *TOPEKA Magazine*. She writes and illustrates children's books, including *The Fish's Wishes, Bird*, and *Ting & the Caterbury Tales*, and has had her creative non-fiction included in *105 Meadowlark Reader* and other anthologies. One such work, "Winter Guests," was nominated for a Pushcart Prize. Her poems, "Whisper" and "Silence" were published online at 150kansaspoems.wordpress.com. A fiction piece, "The Critique," was published in a recent issue of *The Pen Woman*.

-103-

www.ingramcontent.com/pod-product-compliance
Lightning Source LLC
Chambersburg PA
CBHW071202300726
48975CB00004B/1260